ACHIEVING SPEECH & LANGUAGE TARGETS

ACHIEVING SPEECH & LANGUAGE TARGETS

CATHERINE **DELAMAIN**
& JILL **SPRING**

Speechmark

Throughout the book the child is referred to as 'he' for the sake of simplicity.

First published in 2007 by

Speechmark Publishing Ltd, 70 Alston Drive, Bradwell Abbey, Milton Keynes MK13 9HG, UK
Tel: +44 (0) 1908 326 944   Fax: +44 (0) 1908 326 960
www.speechmark.net

Reprinted 2009

002-5333/Printed in the United Kingdom/1010

British Library Cataloguing in Publication Data

Delamain, Catherine
    Achieving speech and language targets : a resource for individual education
    planning 1. Language arts (Elementary) – Great Britain.   2. English language –
    Study and teaching (Elementary) – Great Britain   3. Oral communication –
    Study and teaching (Elementary) – Great Britain   4. Individualized instruction –
    Great Britain
    I. Title   II. Spring, Jill
    372.6'044'0941

ISBN: 978 0 86388 579 2

Contents

CONTENTS

Acknowledgements

Grateful thanks to Mrs Sarah Goddard, Senior Educational Psychologist for Dorset Education Authority, from whom we have learnt so much and who gave much wise advice during the planning of this book.

Thanks also to the many teachers and children who over the years have enabled us to advance our knowledge of language and communication.

Preface

Special needs co-ordinators (SENCOs), teachers and teaching assistants in primary and first schools are regularly required to implement Individual Education Plans (IEPs) provided by speech and language therapists. Equally often special needs co-ordinators or class teachers need to draw up their own IEPs to address the early stages of a speech or language teaching programme. They may also find it necessary to amplify, clarify or simplify existing IEPs.

This book aims to provide teachers and speech & language therapists with a shared reference, from which broad special needs areas and specific targets can be identified. The targets reflect the concerns most often voiced by both teachers and therapists. The book offers a wide range of detailed activities to help children achieve their targets. Many of the activities can take place in the context of the everyday curriculum, and include a range of play opportunities designed to make learning interesting and dynamic. Almost all can be carried out with the equipment available in early years classrooms, and be delivered by teaching assistants with the minimum of explanation.

The activities aim to meet the needs of the majority of children with speech or language delay from school entry at 4 years plus, up to the end of the first year of formal education. They can of course also be used with children who do not have Individual Education Plans (IEPs), but who are seen as needing a speech and language enhancement programme. They will also be appropriate for children for whom English is an additional language.

Although the authors have made reference to the National Curriculum of England and Wales, the activities are not dependent on knowledge or experience of the National Curriculum and can be carried out by any English-speaking user.

This book offers:

- guidance on drawing up and working with IEPs, using the checklists to help identify problems.
- an extensive list of games and activities linked to special educational needs areas
- a resources section.

Introduction

Teaching and learning are principally mediated through speech and language. Good communication skills are therefore fundamental to successful learning. This book emphasises the crucial role of play in language development. Recent initiatives in the UK such as the SEAL project (Social and Emotional Aspects of Learning), Sure Start and Excellence and Enjoyment also recognise that social skills, emotional security and good communication set the scene for later learning.

Speech and language difficulties account for one of the largest groups of young children needing remediation. In any Reception or Key Stage 1 classroom in the UK at least 10 per cent of children are likely to have significant deficits in one or both areas. Some children start school with the speech and language levels of two-year-olds and there is an increasing number of children for whom English is a second language. Teachers struggle to reconcile the demands of the National Curriculum with the needs of children for whom the development of communication is the overriding priority.

This book is founded on the belief that a fundamental element of language learning in young children involves play with an adult. Many children have missed the concentrated language input ideally provided by parents and carers which focuses on the child's play and interests, and is characterised by immediacy, simplicity and repetition. It is therefore crucial that foundation stage teachers are prepared to include adult–child play as a vital component of the curriculum.

The book offers teachers and SENCOs guidance on the use of adult–child play to further children's language learning in an easily accessible structured format. It includes:

- a guide to appropriate play levels
- a range of teaching activities
- a resources section linking to the activities including suggested techniques, activity sheets, games and rhymes, a booklist, a list of suppliers and a dictionary of terms used in relation to speech and language.

How to use this book

LAYOUT

The book is divided into four parts:

- Activities for Understanding Language (Part I)
- Activities for Using Language (Part II)
- Activities for Developing Speech Sounds (Part III)
- Resources (Part IV)

The symbol denotes materials you will need for the teaching target.

Activities for Understanding Language

This part focuses on developing a child's understanding of spoken language, from basic vocabulary to simple stories. A checklist at the beginning of each section helps to identify areas of the child's speech and language difficulties. Each of the ten activity sections includes:

- An Activity Area list which indicates the most suitable types of activity for that particular stage
- Examples of key vocabulary or sentence type
- Teaching Ideas

Activities for Using Language

This part focuses on developing the child's ability to use spoken language, from basic vocabulary to simple sentences and questions. At the beginning is a checklist to help identify areas of the child's speech and language difficulties. Each of the five activity sections includes:

- An Activity Area list which indicates the most suitable types of activity for that particular stage
- Examples of key vocabulary or sentence type
- Teaching Ideas

Activities for Developing Speech Sounds

This part aims to teach children to identify, make and use new speech sounds. A checklist at the beginning helps to identify areas of the child's speech difficulties. It includes an introduction, developmental information and learning steps.

Resources

This part includes:

- Games and Rhymes – a range of traditional, commercial and specific games and a number of useful rhymes

- Techniques – an explanation of the techniques referred to in the Activity sections

- Photocopiable Activity sheets

- A useful list of books, suppliers and commercial games

- Dictionary of simple definitions of terms that refer to speech and language

IDENTIFYING SPEECH AND LANGUAGE DIFFICULTIES

Checklists for Understanding Language, Using Spoken Language and Developing Speech Sounds can be found at the beginning of Parts I, II and III. The checklists cover a range of speech and language difficulties from an approximate developmental age of 2.5 years to 5.00 years. These are divided into four stages which link to P Scales 5/6 – National Curriculum Level 1.

The problems identified on the checklists are those most likely to have an impact on the child's social, emotional and educational progress. In addition they are the ones frequently identified by speech & language therapists. The authors acknowledge that progression through the stages sometimes involves very large developmental steps. However, an attempt has been made to target the key skills necessary to meet the demands of the National Curriculum Level 1.

Using the checklists

When a child's communication skills are causing concern, photocopy the checklists at the start of Parts I, II and III. Go through each checklist, highlighting areas of delay with reference to the child's actual age. In some instances you will see that activities only start at Stage Two (for example, colour), because the skill is not always achieved until this stage in normal development.

It is important to look at all three checklists. A child may have delays in one or more areas. Speech difficulties and difficulties with using spoken language are usually easy to identify, while problems with understanding may be less obvious. It is vital that a child understands a word or sentence type before being taught to use it himself. Similarly he must have adequate use of language before tackling speech sounds.

Choose not more than three priorities to start work on. They may all focus on one area, for example, understanding language, or be spread across two or all three areas (using language and/or developing speech sounds). Map these priorities on to the child's IEP (teaching programme). You will need to return to the checklists when planning new IEPs. You can also use the checklists to record broad areas of achievement and to ensure that the child is making even progress.

WORKING WITH INDIVIDUAL EDUCATION PLANS (IEPs)

Most children with special educational needs will have an IEP. This is a document which outlines a child's broad areas of difficulty and describes the way in which these difficulties are to be addressed. The layout and wording of IEPs will differ from school to school but all speech and language IEPs should include:

- the main areas of difficulty (for example, very poor understanding of position words)
- specific short-term targets (for example, will understand meaning of *in front/ behind*)
- activities, resources and teaching staff involved

The success of an IEP will depend on how carefully the specific short-term targets are designed. Many teachers and teaching assistants will be familiar with the term SMART target. The letters S M A R T refer to the criteria for an effective IEP. Targets should be:

- **S**pecific
- **M**easurable
- **A**chievable
- **R**elevant
- **T**ime limited

Specific ▶ the target should describe a particular activity which will reflect the aims as identified on the checklist.

Measurable ▶ the target should include an outcome which can be easily verified.

Achievable ▶ the target needs to be realistically achievable, based on the child's ability and the adult's expectations.

Relevant ▶ the target needs to be meaningful, functionally useful and relevant to current classroom and curricular demands.

Time limited ▶ when setting the target a time frame must be specified in order to monitor outcomes effectively.

The following table shows examples of unhelpful and helpful (SMART) targets.

UNHELPFUL TARGETS	SMART TARGETS
Connor will know his colours	In 6 weeks Connor will be able to point to the red, blue or green balloon when asked
Connor will use plurals	In 4 weeks Connor will be able to use the plural /s/ to indicate the difference between single objects and groups of objects or pictures
Milly will speak more clearly	By July Milly will always use the correct sound at the beginning of /c/k/ words when naming pictures
Nassim will know more position words	By the end of term Nassim will be able to stand *beside*, *between*, *near* other people when told in PE/gym

Example of a Typical IEP for a Child with a Language Difficulty

DATE OF IEP ——————————— CHILD ———————————

CLASS ——————————— DATE OF REVIEW ———————————

BASELINE	TARGET	SCHOOL ACTION		SCHOOL ACTION PLUS/STATEMENT	OUTCOME MEASURES
Only understands Stage One position words	By half term child will respond accurately to instructions involving in front of, away, behind	Include commands with target position words in PE	Receptive position words Stage Two three times weekly either 1:1 or small group	SLT monitors progress and updates as necessary	Can respond appropriately to in front of, away, behind in a structured play activity. Does not always respond to same instructions in class
Does not understand early descriptive words	By July will be able to choose between big and little pairs of objects on command		Choose activities from Understanding Describing Words Stage 1 – 1:1 or small group work with TA 2 x weekly		Can respond appropriately in a structured situation but not always reliably in class

Please note that words such as *know, understand* are not easily measurable and therefore do not make SMART targets. Useful words include *show, point to, follow, identify, name, say, pronounce.*

PLANNING THE ACTIVITIES

Having identified areas to work on and described your specific targets, you are ready to plan activities to achieve them. Refer to the relevant page in the Activity section.

1 The **Activity Area** list heading each section suggests the types of play and other activities suitable for that developmental level. A list of activity areas and their related stages is given on the next page. This provides an at-a-glance summary of what resources are used for each stage. *When planning your own activities it is important to keep the development of play progression in mind.* For example, a child working at Stage One, P Scale 5-6, age equivalent 2/3, will be most appropriately taught through parallel play in the Home Corner, and practical activities such as Sand & Water.

2 The **vocabulary boxes** at the beginning of each stage in Parts I and II give examples of vocabulary and sentences typical of this level of development. The child may have mastered some of these already and you will want to add others as necessary. Where references are made to specific techniques (for example parallel play) these are explained in the alphabetical **list of techniques** in Resources (pp228–30). *It is important to understand a technique before embarking on any activity that involves its use.*

3 You will see that Part III, Developing Speech Sounds, follows a different format from Parts I and II and includes introductory guidance and normative information.

Most of the activities can be adapted for use with a single child or a small group. The teaching ideas are intended as starting points for developing further activities relevant to the individual child. It will often be necessary to teach the targets in many different ways to consolidate learning. This may include direct one-to-one teaching, small group work and general class activities. Success criteria should be implicit in an IEP, but where no IEP is involved it is vitally important to check for secure learning at frequent intervals.

If the child is finding difficulty with the stage he is working at, drop back to the previous stage. Once the child has mastered a task it may be appropriate to work on further targets within that stage, or perhaps to move on to the next stage.

ACTIVITY AREAS
IN DEVELOPMENTAL ORDER

These activity areas are listed in developmental order. Work out which activities match the stage you are working at. For example, at Stage One the types of activity range from Home Corner to Circle Games.

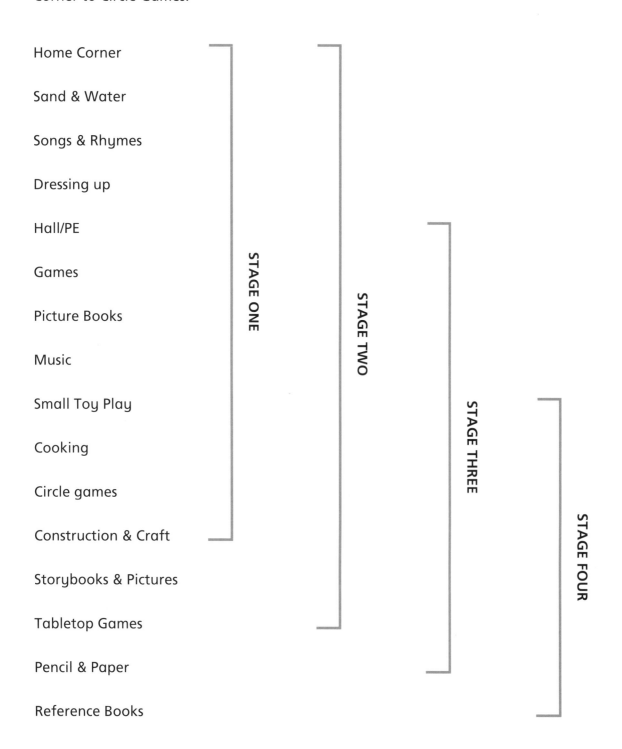

Home Corner

Sand & Water

Songs & Rhymes

Dressing up

Hall/PE

Games

Picture Books

Music

Small Toy Play

Cooking

Circle games

Construction & Craft

Storybooks & Pictures

Tabletop Games

Pencil & Paper

Reference Books

STAGE ONE

STAGE TWO

STAGE THREE

STAGE FOUR

PART I ACTIVITIES FOR UNDERSTANDING LANGUAGE

CHECKLIST FOR PART I: UNDERSTANDING LANGUAGE

	P Scale 5/6 Stage One 2–3 years equivalent	P Scale 6/7 Stage Two 3–4 years equivalent	P Scale 7/8 Stage Three 4–4.5 years equivalent	NC Level 1+ Stage Four 4.5–5 years equivalent
NAMING WORDS (nouns)	Does not understand the names for most familiar things in his world	Naming vocabulary limited to familiar everyday things	Vocabulary still weak. Does not know names for groups of items (eg animals, food)	Does not know narrower category words (eg fruit, vegetables)
ACTION WORDS (verbs)	Does not understand words for familiar actions, (eg jump, run, wash, drink)	Does not understand action words used in class (eg cut, draw, stick)	Does not understand abstract verbs (eg choose, guess, pretend)	Does not understand verbs used in curriculum (eg compare, arrange, estimate)
DESCRIBING WORDS (adjectives)	Does not understand early descriptive words (eg big, little, naughty, good, fast)	Does not understand next descriptive words (eg cold, dry, soft, full)	Does not understand further words for size, texture, quality (eg short, rough)	Does not understand more abstract descriptive words (eg early, late, solid, liquid)
POSITION WORDS (prepositions of place)	Does not understand words that describe position (eg in, on, under)	Does not understand later position words (eg behind, in front of)	Does not understand harder position words (eg beside, through, between, near)	Does not understand advanced position words (eg above, below, face to face, opposite)
COLOURS	It is acceptable for children at this developmental level not to know colours	Knows no colour names, or only one or two	Does not know all basic colour names	
QUESTIONS	Does not understand early question words (eg What? Which?)	Does not understand Who/Where? questions	Does not understand When/Why? questions	Does not understand How can you tell? and How do you make? questions

	P Scale 5/6 Stage One 2–3 years equivalent	P Scale 6/7 Stage Two 3–4 years equivalent	P Scale 7/8 Stage Three 4–4.5 years equivalent	NC Level 1+ Stage Four 4.5–5 years equivalent
QUANTITY WORDS	Does not understand early words for quantity (eg *lots, more, a little bit, too many, no more*)	Does not understand further words for quantity (eg *all of, another, some of, enough*)	Does not understand harder quantity words (eg *more than, less than, fewer, how many*)	Does not understand more complex quantity words (eg *either/or, all/except, exact, about right, each, every other, altogether*)
SENTENCES AND INSTRUCTIONS	Cannot understand sentences with three main information words (eg *Daddy's reading a book*)	Cannot follow sentences with four main information words (eg *Daddy's reading Sally's book*)	Cannot follow two-step instructions	Cannot follow instructions with three main ideas (eg *Put your books away, get your coats and line up.*)
TIME WORDS	Does not understand early time words (eg *now, in a minute, soon, morning, night*)	Does not understand next time words (eg *today, tomorrow, after, birthday*)	Does not understand harder words about time (eg *yesterday, later, days of the week*)	Does not understand further time words (eg *always, sometimes, usually, never, evening, long ago*)
STORIES	Does not attend to simplest stories	Cannot follow a simple storyline accompanied by pictures	Cannot follow a story with few pictures	Cannot understand the main theme of a more complicated story or explanation Cannot make inferences – understand something implied but not spelt out

UNDERSTANDING NAMING WORDS
STAGE ONE

ACTIVITY AREAS
- ▶ Songs & rhymes
- ▶ Home Corner
- ▶ Games
- ▶ Construction & craft
- ▶ Small toy play
- ▶ Picture books

VOCABULARY

Myself	eyes, nose, mouth, feet, hands, hair, fingers
Clothes	child's everyday clothes
People	man, lady (woman), boy, girl, baby
Household	bed, chair, table, cup, spoon, plate
Food	apple, orange, juice, milk, biscuit, bread, sandwich
Vehicles	car, bus, bike, taxi
Animals	cat, dog, horse, cow, pig, rabbit
Inside	kitchen, bathroom, bedroom, living room, toilet
Outside	field, gate, house
Toys	brick, ball, sand, water
Craft items	pencils, paper, paints, glue, scissors

WHAT TO DO

The vocabulary list in the box is just a start, and gives you an idea of the sort of words to teach at this stage. You can add other early naming words as they crop up.

- Choose up to four or five words from one or more word groups, provided they can be conveniently taught together.

- Choose one of the activities suggested below, or plan your own activity by adapting one of them.

- Work your way through the vocabulary list a few at a time. You may have to teach some of the words in several different ways on several different occasions.

- Examples of useful books can be found in Resources, pp261–2.

TEACHING IDEAS

(1) TEACHING TARGET: to understand *hands/fingers* (Myself)

▶ **Songs & rhymes**

 The words of the action rhyme One Little Finger (Resources, p226)

Ask the children to show you their *hands*, demonstrating as necessary. Hold up one *finger* and encourage the children to copy you. Sing or chant the action rhyme. When you use this or other action rhymes to teach parts of the body, go very slowly at first, making sure the child is making the action or pointing to the right part of the body as you say the words.

(2) TEACHING TARGET: to understand *bed, chair, cups, table* (Household)

▶ **Home Corner**

 Big teddies, dolls, beds, chairs, table, teaset

Parallel play, joining the children in getting the toys up and putting them to *bed*. ('I think teddy wants to go to sleep. I'm putting him in the *bed*.' 'Your doll can sit on this *chair*.' 'We can put these *cups* on the *table*.') Parallel play in the Home Corner is a useful way of teaching lots of Stage One vocabulary.

(3) TEACHING TARGET: to understand *apples, oranges, biscuits, bread, sandwich* (Food)

▶ **Home Corner**

 Big teddies, dolls, tables and chairs, teaset, toy food

Parallel play, joining the children to give the toys a party. ('This teddy wants an *apple*. Here you are, teddy.' 'I think your teddy likes *oranges* best.' 'Dolly has got a *biscuit*.')

(4) TEACHING TARGET: to understand *horse, cow, dog, cat* (Animals and Outside)

▶ **Small toy play**

 Toy farm, animals

Join the children in setting out the farm, making the animals walk into and out of the barns and fields. ('I'm putting this *horse* in the field.' 'Here's another *horse*'. 'You've got the big *cow*.' 'A *dog* is coming. Look, here he comes.')

5 **TEACHING TARGET: to remember several different toy names (Toys)**

▶ **Games**

 A feely bag made of some soft material and a collection of toys small enough to go into the bag

Talk about the toys with the children, naming all of them more than once. Then put one into the feely bag without the children seeing what it is. Let one child have a good feel of the bag and try to guess what is inside it. Pull the toy out. Were they right? Name the toy again, and repeat with another toy and another child.

6 **TEACHING TARGET: to understand *pencil, paper, paint, finger, foot, hand* (Craft items and Myself)**

▶ **Construction & craft**

 Pencil, paper and paints

Look at the *pencil*, *paper* and *paints*, talking about them, using their names as you do so. Spread the child's *hand* out on the *paper* and draw round the shape, outlining the *fingers*. Lift up his *hand* and show him. 'Look! That's your *hand*. And here are your *fingers* – one *finger*, two *fingers*.' Stand him on the *paper* and draw round his *foot*. 'See, here's your *foot*.' Help him *paint* the shapes of his *hand* and *foot*.

7 **TEACHING TARGET: to remember some of the naming words already introduced, eg *pencil, sock, horse, apple***

▶ **Games**

 Two of each of the items you have chosen and a box

Hide one of each pair of objects around the room, keeping the second one in your box. In turn, send the children off to find an item ('John, find me a *pencil*. Jamilla, find me a *sock*.') If the child looks doubtful, show him the matching item you have in your box. If a child comes back with the wrong item, show him what he should have found and stress its name again ('You needed to find a *sock* like this.')

8 **TEACHING TARGET: to remember some of the naming words already introduced, eg *jumper, sock, shoe, shirt, trousers* (Clothes)**

▶ **Picture books**

 A suitable picture book

Choose a book with single, large, clear, coloured pictures. Go through the book with the child, naming the pictures. Where possible, relate the pictures to the real thing, in this case his own or others' clothes. ('It's like your *jumper*, isn't it? And those *shoes* are like Bobby's *shoes*, look.')

> *Wherever possible, the child should experience handling real or toy objects in one of the other activity areas, before moving on to identifying them in picture books.*

UNDERSTANDING NAMING WORDS
STAGE TWO

ACTIVITY AREAS

▶ Songs & rhymes
▶ Dressing up/Home Corner
▶ Small toy play

▶ Games
▶ Construction & craft
▶ Tabletop games
▶ Storybooks

VOCABULARY

Myself	lips, tongue, head, teeth, chin, knee, shoulder, toes
Clothes	boots, hat, anorak, vest, sandals, gloves, scarf
People	postman, policeman, doctor, nurse, dentist, teacher
Household	phone, cooker, kettle, clock, fridge, sink, TV, sofa, cupboard
Food	eggs, beans, cake, carrot, banana, jam
Vehicles	plane, helicopter, tractor, motorbike, lorry, train
Animals	fish, hamster, bird, spider, elephant, giraffe, camel
Inside	walls, stairs, curtains, carpets, doors, picture
Outside	trees, roads, shops, garage, station, park, farm
Toys	Lego, skipping rope, roller skates, kite, swing, slide
Craft items	ruler, rubber, glue, scissors
Weather	rain, wind, sun, ice, snow, frost

WHAT TO DO

The vocabulary list in the box is just a start, and gives you an idea of the sort of words to teach at this stage. You can add other naming words as they crop up or become necessary.

- Choose up to four or five words from one or more groups, provided they can conveniently be taught together.

- Choose one of the activities suggested below, or plan your own activity by adapting one of them.

- Examples of useful books can be found in Resources, pp261–2.

TEACHING IDEAS

1 **TEACHING TARGET: to understand head, *shoulders, knees, toes* (Myself)**

▶ **Songs & rhymes**

The words of the action rhyme 'Heads, Shoulders, Knees and Toes' (Resources, p224)

Sing or chant the rhyme. Go very slowly at first, pointing to each feature as it is named and waiting until the children are all pointing to the right spot. Only speed up when the names are learnt and you can just have fun. Another good rhyme at this stage is 'One Finger, One Thumb' (Resources, p226).

2 **TEACHING TARGET: to understand *doctor, nurse, boy, girl* (People)**

▶ **Dressing up/Home Corner**

Doctor and nurse outfits, teddies, dolls, beds

Extended play. Join the children in their play and encourage some role play, either tending sick teddies and dolls or having one or more children as the professionals and one or more as the patients. ('I think teddy is sick. Come on, *nurse*, let's put him to bed here. I think we need the *doctor*. Can the *doctor* give him some medicine? This *boy* has fallen over and hurt himself.')

3 **TEACHING TARGET: to understand *elephant, giraffe, camel* (Animals)**

▶ **Small toy play**

Zoo animals (at least two of each), toy zoo or playmat

Extended play. Guide the children towards the idea of finding two of each animal, or several, or finding mother and baby animals. ('Look, I've found a baby *camel*. Can you see the mother *camel*?' 'That's an *elephant* you've got. Here, I've got another *elephant*.')

4 **TEACHING TARGET: to understand *eggs, beans, cake, carrots, bananas* (Food)**

▶ **Games**

 A collection of food pictures, several of each item, and a container

Put all the pictures into the container, and give the children turns to pull out one picture. The child names the picture if he can, otherwise you name it for him, and he says if he likes it or not. If he doesn't like it, it goes back into the container. If he does, he keeps it in front of him. When everyone has a small collection, take turns to tell each other what your favourite meal consists of, as represented by the pictures you have collected. It may be rather a strange mixture! Help with the food names as much as necessary.

> *It is important where possible that the children have seen the real thing before using pictures of food.*

5 **TEACHING TARGET: to understand *cooker, fridge, sink, sofa, television* (Household)**

▶ **Small toy play**

 Doll's house, miniature dolls, doll's house furniture

Extended play. Encourage the children to put appropriate furniture in the various rooms. ('Where do you think this *fridge* should go? Shall I put it in the kitchen?' 'Look, Mum can sit on the *settee*. She's watching the *TV.*')

6 **TEACHING TARGET: to understand *rain* (Weather)**

▶ **Construction & craft**

 A large sheet of paper, a sheet of paper for each child, crayons, scissors and glue

Show the children how to draw simple shapes as raindrops, colour them in and cut them out. Then help them stick their raindrops all over the top of your large sheet. You could add a pond, a puddle and somebody with boots and an umbrella. Talk about the *rain*, how it makes things wet, how it splashes in puddles. Talk about what you need to wear when it's *rainy* – mac, boots (wellies) a hat or hood.

> *Before working on weather words in this way, wherever possible take the children to experience the real thing first. Go out and feel the rain on your hands, watch it splashing in the pond, watch the raindrops coming down the windowpane, and use the words 'rain' and 'raining' repeatedly.*

7 **TEACHING TARGET: to understand** *plane, helicopter, motorbike, lorry, train* **(Vehicles)**

▶ **Tabletop games**

 Two identical sets of picture cards showing vehicles

Shuffle the two packs together. Play the Pairs (Resources, p219) game, either you with one child or two children together. The child turns two pictures over and you name the pictures. Encourage the child to say the names. If you think the child nearly knows the word, prompt by giving him the first sound ('It's a p...') or by giving him an association ('It runs on a track'). Other good tabletop games are Picture Dominoes and Picture Lotto (Resources, pp219, 220).

8 **TEACHING TARGET: to understand** *skipping rope, kite, swing, slide* **(Toys)**

▶ **Storybooks**

 A suitable storybook

Choose a simple story about going to the play park. Read the story with the children, stopping often to show the pictures and name them. ('Tom loved the *slide* and went on it lots of times – look, here's the *slide*.' 'This girl's flying a *kite* – hold on tight little girl.') Go through the pictures again, asking the child to point to the target words.

Wherever possible the child should have direct experience of playing with this sort of equipment before moving on to hearing about it in storybooks.

UNDERSTANDING NAMING WORDS
STAGE THREE

ACTIVITY AREAS

▶ Small toy play
▶ Construction & craft
▶ Storybooks

▶ Tabletop games
▶ Games

VOCABULARY AND CATEGORY NAMES

Body	ankle, elbow, chest, wrist, neck
Jobs	builder, plumber, policeman, shopkeeper, engineer
Furniture	cupboard, wardrobe, chest, stool, bunk bed
Vehicles, transport	van, moped, boat, liner, yacht
Creatures	goat, duck, goose, hippo, seal, beetle, goldfish
Sports and games	football, rugby, tennis, swimming, chess, skating
Buildings	houses, flats, offices, castles, barns, stables
Food	lemons, grapefruit, cabbage, lettuce, meat, butter, pies, sausages, bacon
Seasons	spring, summer, autumn, winter

WHAT TO DO

The aim at Stage Three is not only to teach the *category names* (Vehicles, Sports, Seasons, Jobs etc.), it is also an opportunity to introduce lots of new words in each category. This may tie in well with current topics. Add as many new words to each category as needed and as time permits.

- Work your way through the categories, including both earlier words and new ones. Use teaching ideas 1–5 below, or plan your own activities by adapting them. Once you have worked on three to four categories, try activities 6–8.

- As you may be introducing a lot of new vocabulary, don't expect the children to remember it after only one or two games. You may have to go over things in several different ways on several different occasions.

- Examples of useful books can be found in Resources, pp261–2.

TEACHING IDEAS

1 **TEACHING TARGET: to understand the word and concept of Furniture and harder words in this category (*cupboard, wardrobe, chest, stool, bunk bed*)**

▶ **Small toy play**

Doll's house, doll's house furniture

Extended play. Ask the children to take all the *furniture* out of the house. Give them time to play with it and talk about it as they do so. Name all the unfamiliar items for them. Have they got a *wardrobe* like that at home? Does anyone sleep in a *bunk bed* like this one? Use the word *furniture* repeatedly. When they have got it all out, say 'What a lot of *furniture* you've found.'

2 **TEACHING TARGET: to understand the word and concept of Food and harder words in this category (*lemons, grapefruit, meat, butter, pies, bacon*)**

▶ **Construction & craft**

A large scrapbook, some old catalogues or magazines, scissors and glue

Tell the children they are going to make a book of *food*. Set them to look through the magazines and cut out as many *food* items as they can find. Give them five minutes, and make a challenge of it to see how many items they can find in that time. When they have a good collection, help them stick their pictures into the scrapbook. As well as naming all the items, use the word *food* repeatedly ('What a lot of different kinds of *food* you've found.')

3 **TEACHING TARGET: to understand the word and concept of *summer* (Seasons)**

▶ **Storybooks**

A story about a summer activity, for example going to the beach

Tell the children you are going to talk about one of the *seasons* – the different times in the year. The *season* in this story is *summer*. Talk about the things that happen in the *summer* – we wear cooler clothes, we may go swimming, we may go on holiday. Read the story, stopping often to point out things that are special to *summer*. Make sure everyone can see the pictures. At the end, remind them that it was a story about *summer* – one of the *seasons* of the year.

④ TEACHING TARGET: to understand the word and concept of a _builder_ (Jobs)

▶ **Story books**

A suitable story book about builders

Tell the children you are going to learn about some _jobs_ that people do. This one is a _builder_ – he makes houses, shops, flats and offices. Does anybody know someone who is a _builder_? Read bits of the book to the children, simplifying the language where necessary and sticking to basic facts. Show all the pictures and explain what is happening. Use the word _builder_ frequently and encourage discussion and questions. At the end, remind the children you were talking about _jobs_ people do – this man's job was a _builder_.

⑤ TEACHING TARGET: to understand the word and concept of Creatures and harder words in this category (_goat, duck, goose, hippopotamus, beetle, goldfish_)

▶ **Games**

Find or cut out lots of animal, bird, fish and insect pictures. You also need fishing rods from one of the commercial fishing games, paper clips and a wide-mouthed box or other container. Attach a paper clip to each picture and put the pictures in the container.

Tell the children you are going to fish out a lot of _creatures_. The children take turns to fish them out. Help them with the names if necessary, and use the word _creatures_ repeatedly. You might make this game more fun by allocating a number to each creature and seeing whose creatures add up to the biggest number at the end. You might put in a couple of joke pictures like a boot and a chair.

> _Activities like the next three should be played when you have worked on several categories and those category names are familiar. Start with the most familiar ones._

6 **TEACHING TARGET: to remember the category names Vehicles (Transport) and Food**

▶ **Tabletop games**

A collection of food pictures and a collection of vehicle pictures

Decide whether you are going to use the word 'vehicles' or 'transport' or whether to use them interchangeably. Mix the pictures up and spread them out face up on the table. This game can be played by one child, two children, or four children working in pairs. Allocate a category to each child or pair. ('You are looking for all the *food*.' 'You are looking for all the *vehicles*.') Give each child or pair a 'guide' picture (a *food* item to one, and a *vehicle* to the other), so there is no doubt about what they are looking for. Say 'Ready, steady, go' and see how long they take to find all the pictures in their respective categories. Check for mistakes at the end and sort them out. Reinforce that they were sorting *food* and *vehicles*.

7 **TEACHING TARGET: to remember the names of three or four categories worked on**

▶ **Tabletop games**

Several pictures from each of your chosen categories

Mix up the pictures and deal out four pictures, face down, to each child playing. Put one picture from each category face up on the table. Call out a category name, eg *creatures*. The children turn up their top card, and if they think they have a *creature* they put up their hand. If they are right, their card goes down on the table on top of the *creature* picture. Continue play until everyone has got rid of all their cards. You can make it into a competition by letting the first child to get rid of his cards be the winner.

8 **TEACHING TARGET: to be able to remember the names of three or four categories**

▶ **Tabletop games**

Several pictures from each of your chosen categories, a timer

Scatter the pictures face up in the middle of the table. Allocate each child a category and tell them it is a race to see who can collect all the items in his category first. Say 'Ready, steady, go' – and start the timer. At the end, see if there are any unclaimed pictures. Whose collection should they belong to? Check for confusions or errors.

UNDERSTANDING NAMING WORDS
STAGE FOUR

ACTIVITY AREAS

- ▶ Small toy play
- ▶ Games
- ▶ Construction & craft
- ▶ Storybooks
- ▶ Tabletop games
- ▶ Reference books

VOCABULARY AND NARROW CATEGORY NAMES

mammals	trees
fish	fruit
reptiles	vegetables
insects/minibeasts	meat
birds	dairy
flowers	tools

WHAT TO DO

The aim at Stage Four is to teach the category names and also to introduce lots of new words in each category. There are many other subcategories you may want to include now or at a later stage.

- Work your way through the categories, including both earlier words and new ones. Use the teaching ideas 1–5 below, or plan your own activities by adapting them. Add as many new words as needed and as time permits.

- Once you have worked on three or four categories, try teaching ideas 6–8.

- Examples of useful books can be found in Resources, pp261–2.

TEACHING IDEAS

1 **TEACHING TARGET: to understand the word and concept of Fruit and new words in this category**

▶ **Small toy play**

 Toy fruit

Tell the children you are going to be talking about *fruit*. Name any unfamiliar ones for the children. (If at all possible, try to bring in examples of unfamiliar fruits to show them.) Select a fruit, name it and pass it round to the children in turn, asking them to say something about it. Prompt and help, or offer ideas, as necessary. (Examples: it tastes sweet, it grows on a tree/bush, you can peel it, you can make puddings [desserts] with it, you can put sugar and cream on it, it's good for you, it has pips/seeds.) Repeat with other fruits, remembering to keep reinforcing the names of new ones. Accept single-word or very brief ideas from children with speech or expressive language difficulties. At the end, talk about the things *fruits* have in common – they grow on trees or bushes, they are sweet, you eat them raw or in desserts.

2 **TEACHING TARGET: to understand the word and concept of Dairy, and words in this category**

▶ **Games**

 Food pictures, including as many dairy products as possible, pictures of cows, goats and sheep, and a picture of both bottles and cartons of milk

It may still be necessary to explain to some children that milk comes from cows, goats and sheep. Select a child to be the *dairy* farmer, the person who looks after the animals, and tell them that all the *dairy products* come from milk. The children are to try to guess which of the food pictures might be made by the *dairy* farmer, and put them in front of him. It won't be fruit, vegetables or meat – so what's left? As they choose pictures, help them decide whether they are right (cheese of all kinds, cream, butter, yoghurt, various readymade milk desserts).

3 **TEACHING TARGET: to understand the word and concept of Flowers and some flower names**

▶ **Construction & craft**

 A scrapbook, some tissue paper, flower heads from different plants

This collection may not be easy to achieve in a town, but if a few children can bring in at least one flower head from a bunch in a vase or from a windowbox, five or six will do. Name the flowers. Talk about *flowers* in general, that they are grown for their beauty and their scent. Tell the children you are going to make a scrapbook of *flowers*. Help the children press the flowers in tissue paper between two heavy books. On a later occasion, help them stick the flowers into the scrapbook.

④ TEACHING TARGET: to understand the words and concept of Insects and Minibeasts

▶ **Storybooks**

Suitable storybook about minibeasts (for example, *The Very Hungry Caterpillar* by Eric Carle. See booklist in Resources, p261)

Read the story, talking about how the *caterpillar* turns into a *butterfly*. The children will probably have read this story when they were younger. It explains beautifully the stages of life of the butterfly. Help the children think up some more creepie-crawlie minibeasts like the caterpillar – *worms*, *slugs*, *snails*, *woodlice*.

⑤ TEACHING TARGET: to understand the word and concept of Fish and some fish names

▶ **Reference books**

Suitable reference book on fish with good clear pictures

Talk about it with the children, thinking about where the *fish* live, how the *fishermen* catch them, where we can buy *fish* to eat. Has anyone got a *fish*tank at home? What sorts of *fish* are in it? Can they come out of the water? What might happen if they did? Name some of the more usual fish.

> *The next three ideas should be used when you have worked on several categories and their names are familiar.*

⑥ TEACHING TARGET: to understand the word and concept of Vegetables and know some vegetable names

▶ **Tabletop games**

A very large table, a very large area of paper (some wallpaper lining is good) and a collection of all kinds of food pictures

Draw a huge circle on the paper. Ask the children to throw all the food pictures into the circle, and tell them you are putting lots of food in there. Now mark out a single segment in the circle. Help the children push all the pictures, face up and spread out, into the main part of the circle. Now tell them to find all the vegetable pictures and put them into the marked out segment. Discuss how *vegetables* differ from flowers, although they are both plants. Point out that they already know quite a few *vegetables*. Help as much as necessary, but encourage them to discuss their decisions amongst themselves as well. When the sorting is done satisfactorily, point out again that everything in the circle is food, but only the things in the small segment are *vegetables*. (You can build on this game by dividing your circle into three or four sections and sorting the pictures into four groups, eg fruit, vegetables, meat, dairy.)

7 **TEACHING TARGET: to remember and differentiate between Fish, Reptiles and Minibeasts**

▶ **Games**

A 'shop' on a table with an assortment of pictures from the chosen categories and a bag

Tell the children that you are a zookeeper and you are setting up a new zoo. Send the children to fetch you the creatures you ask for from the shop. They should put the item in the bag and bring it to you. ('Shami, please bring me a *reptile*.' 'Ben, please fetch a *minibeast*.') Correct errors immediately. Replace the items brought to you in the 'shop' each time, until everyone has had enough turns, after which you can keep the pictures until the 'shop' is empty. You can turn this game into an auditory memory activity by asking for two or more items at a time ('Please bring me a fish and two reptiles.' 'Please fetch me a reptile, a minibeast, and a fish.')

8 **TEACHING TARGET: to remember several category names and some creatures which belong in them (eg Mammals, Birds, Reptiles and Minibeasts)**

▶ **Reference books**

Some pieces of card, a felt tip pen and a pictorial book on wildlife and habitats

Look at the book together and help the children to find one or two interesting, surprising or unusual facts about mammals, birds, reptiles and minibeasts. Help the children write their interesting fact or facts on the cards. Non-readers can be helped to learn their fact by heart if it is kept short. Ask an obliging adult to act as audience and let the children take turns to present their information. Better still, they can present it to the rest of the class. Each child should introduce his information by saying, 'This is an interesting thing about mammals' or 'This is something about minibeasts.'

UNDERSTANDING ACTION WORDS
STAGE ONE

ACTIVITY AREAS ▶

- ▶ Hall
- ▶ Home Corner
- ▶ Songs & rhymes
- ▶ Construction & craft
- ▶ Games
- ▶ Music

VOCABULARY

come (here)	go	move	run
walk	stand (still/up)	sit (down)	lie (down)
jump	fetch/get	bring	pick (up)
put (down)	hold	carry	lift (up)
eat	drink	wash	dry
brush	blow	sleep	wake up
pull	push	put (on)	take (off)
catch	throw	give	build
knock (down)	fall (down)	cry	laugh
cuddle	smile	kiss	like
want	stop	wait	watch
listen	look (at)	touch	play
find	wave	clap	show

WHAT TO DO

The vocabulary list in the box is just a start to give you an idea of the sort of words to teach at this stage. You can add other early action words as they crop up.

- Choose from the list about five or six words that are suitable to teach together, for example, opposites: give/take; large movements: walk/run; words with similar context: wash, brush, clean, comb, dry.

- Choose one of the activities suggested below, or plan your own activity by adapting one of them.

- Work your way through the vocabulary list a few at a time. You may have to teach some of the words in several different ways on several different occasions.

- Examples of useful books can be found in Resources, pp261–2.

TEACHING IDEAS

1 **TEACHING TARGET: to understand** *run, walk, stop, sit down, stand up*

▶ **Hall**

 None

This activity can be done with only one child, but it is more fun if there are two or three. Play Follow-my-Leader. Tell the children to do what you do. Say '*Walk*', and start walking round the room. Are the children coming behind and copying you? Now say '*Run*', and start running, looking over your shoulder to see if the children are running too. Go back and take the hand of anyone who seems unsure what to do and show him. Continue with '*Stop*', '*Sit down*', '*Stand up*' and repeat the series. It is a great help to have a second adult who can watch the children and demonstrate to them what to do if they seem lost. Once you think the children have learnt the meaning of these words, try putting a child in front as leader and see if he can follow the commands '*Walk*', '*Run*' and so on. Show him if necessary.

2 **TEACHING TARGET: to understand** *throw, catch, give*

▶ **Hall**

 Soft ball or beanbag

This activity needs two or three children. Stand in a circle. Tell the children you are going to *throw* the ball. Call the name of the first child, make sure he is looking at you and say '*Catch*!' When the child has caught the ball, hold out your hands and say '*Throw* to me.' Repeat round the circle. When everyone has had two or three turns, tell the child holding the ball, '*Give* the ball to… (his next-door neighbour.) Show him if necessary and then carry on with the catching and throwing game.

3 **TEACHING TARGET: to understand** *sleep, wake up, lie down, cuddle, kiss*

▶ **Home Corner**

 Big dolls, teddies

Parallel play. Join the children in play with the toys, putting them to bed, getting them up, holding them and giving them a cuddle and a kiss. ('Your doll's fast *asleep*. My teddy's going to *sleep* here. I'll give him a *cuddle* – there. *Lie down*, teddy. Oh, I think your doll's *waking up*.')

④ TEACHING TARGET: to understand *wash, brush, jump, put on*

▶ **Songs & rhymes**

Flannel, brush, towel, hat

You need at least two children. Sing 'Here We Go Round the Mulberry Bush' (Resources, p221), miming the actions yourself and encouraging the children to copy you. ('This is the way we *wash* our face, this is the way we *brush* our hair, this is the way we *dry* ourselves, this is the way we *jump* and *jump*, this is the way we *put on* a hat.') With very young or delayed children, you might want to have a flannel, a brush, a towel and a hat to use for the miming.

⑤ TEACHING TARGET: to understand *build, knock down, fall down, push*

▶ **Construction & craft**

Large bricks or Duplo

Parallel play. Join the children in making towers, putting on as many bricks as they can, pushing the towers and making them fall down. ('I'm going to *build* a really big tower. It's going to *fall* – it's going to *fall down* – whoops! Let's *build* another. Now I can *knock* it *down* – I'll give it a *push*.')

⑥ TEACHING TARGET: to understand *watch, wait, look at, touch, blow*

▶ **Games**

Bubble mixture and a bubble wand

Blow bubbles for the children. As you prepare the wand, say '*Wait*!' (hold up your hand in a waiting gesture), 'Now *watch*!' (get everyone's attention), 'I'm going to *blow*' (blow the bubbles). 'Look at that one!' (point to a particularly big or distant bubble). 'See if you can *touch* one' (demonstrate). When you've blown a few lots, let the children have turns to blow. ('Your turn – *blow*!')

7 **TEACHING TARGET: to understand *listen, look (for), find***

▶ **Games/hall**

Either a battery-operated tape recorder or a toy that makes a continuous noise

Demonstrate the music on the tape recorder, or the sound made by the toy. Tell the children you are going to hide the music or the toy and they are going to *look for* it. Hide the noisemaker and tell the children, 'Open your eyes! Now *listen*! Who can *find* it?' Touch your finger to your ear to indicate listening. Children often have a poor idea of using their ears to trace a sound and tend to rush about using their eyes only. If nobody is showing any signs of finding the noise, start moving gradually towards it, encouraging the children to come with you and reminding them with word and gesture to stop and *listen*.

8 **TEACHING TARGET: to understand *stop, start, wait***

▶ **Music**

A CD/tape recorder, a CD/tape of some lively, rhythmic music, maracas or bells

Give each child an instrument. Start the music and tell them to *start* shaking their instruments in time with the music. Switch off and hold up your hand in the '*Stop*!' gesture, saying '*Stop*!' Repeat the stop/start sequence several times, using words and gestures, and finally stopping the gestures and relying on the verbal commands alone.

UNDERSTANDING ACTION WORDS
STAGE TWO

ACTIVITY AREAS
- ▶ Sand & water
- ▶ Songs & rhymes
- ▶ Hall/PE
- ▶ Games
- ▶ Small toy play
- ▶ Construction & craft

VOCABULARY

climb	ride	drive	kick
skip	hop	tip	fill
pour	cut	fit	write
draw	read	stick	glue
colour	paint	copy	talk
tell	whisper	shout	scream
ask	share	point	show
take	pass	take (turns)	make
turn (on, off, round)	feel	pat	squash
squeeze	roll	bang	shake
tap	dance	swim	race
kneel	start	move	leave (alone)

WHAT TO DO

The vocabulary list in the box is just a start. Add any other words that are particularly appropriate to the child's needs and current classroom activities.

- Choose from the list up to five or six words that are suitable to teach together.

- Choose one of the activities suggested below, or plan your own activity by adapting one of them.

- Work your way through the vocabulary list a few at a time. You may have to teach some of the words in several different ways on several different occasions.

- Examples of useful books can be found in Resources, pp261–2.

TEACHING IDEAS

1 **TEACHING TARGET: to understand *tip, fill, pour, drive***

▶ **Sand**

Buckets, spades, containers and a few toy vehicles

Extended play in the sandpit. Encourage the children to *fill* buckets, *tip* them out to make castles, *pour* sand from one container to another, *drive* toy cars up sandhills. ('Shall we make a big hill? *Fill* your bucket right up. Now *tip* it out on the top – like this. I'm going to *drive* my car right up to the top.')

2 **TEACHING TARGET: to understand *scream, shake, tap, bang***

▶ **Songs & rhymes**

Maracas, drums

Give one instrument to each child. Sing 'Row, Row, Row Your Boat'. Show the children how to *tap* the drums or *shake* the maracas gently until you get to the SCREAM, when they should all *shake* or *bang* loudly and give a *scream*.

3 **TEACHING TARGET: to understand *start, stop, stand still, move***

▶ **Hall/PE**

Radio or tape recorder and lively music

Play the game of Statues (Resources, p223). Tell the children that when the music *starts*, they are to start *moving* about the room. When the music *stops*, they must *stand still* and not move. If necessary, demonstrate this with a confident child or another adult. When the children have got the idea, move among them as they stand still, checking to see if anyone moves. ('Laura, I think you *moved*. You go and sit down. Is Jack *moving*?').

4 **TEACHING TARGET: to understand *hop***

▶ **Hall**

Chalk a very simple hopscotch grid on the floor

Show the children how to *hop* from one box to another. Who can get to the end without putting his second foot down? ('Your turn to *hop*, Sammy. *Hop – hop* – that's right. Oh dear, you put your foot down! You're out.')

5 **TEACHING TARGET: to understand *take, pass, stop, start* and one or two other action words you have worked on**

▶ **Games**

 Beanbag, radio or CD/tape recorder and music, some pictures of actions that are easy to mime

Seat the children in a circle and set the music going. Start off the game by giving one of the children the beanbag. He must *pass* it to his next-door neighbour and so on round the group until the music *stops*. When the music stops, give an action picture to the child who is holding the beanbag. See if he can carry out the action. Can the others guess what he is supposed to be doing? Help as much as necessary. When the action has been guessed, the music starts again and the beanbag goes on its way round the circle. Continue until everyone has had a turn.

6 **TEACHING TARGET: to understand *pull, push, drive, ride***

▶ **Small toy play**

 Toy vehicles and people, Playmobil, farm items

Extended play. Make the tractors *pull* and *push* trailers, the people *drive* the vehicles and *ride* on the trailers. ('Let's hitch this trailer on here. Now the tractor can *pull* the trailer. This man wants to *drive* the tractor.')

7 **TEACHING TARGET: to understand *squeeze, pat, squash, roll, cut***

▶ **Construction & craft**

 Playdough or modelling clay, rolling pin and shape cutters

Extended play making balls, sausage shapes, pancakes. ('Let's *roll* our playdough out flat. Keep *rolling*. Now I'm going to *cut* out a star. Try to *squash* that bit with your hand. We can *roll* this bit into a sausage.')

8 **TEACHING TARGET: to understand *fit (in), find, take turns, share, pass***

▶ **Construction & craft**

 A big floor jigsaw puzzle

Tell the children you are going to *share* the job of making the puzzle. Help them start it off. Once the puzzle is partly done, the children must *take turns* to try and *fit* a piece in. Continue to give as much help as necessary. ('William, try and *fit* this bit in – try here. Now it's Pete's *turn* – here you are, Pete. Does it *fit* there? See if you can *find* the right bit.')

UNDERSTANDING ACTION WORDS
STAGE THREE

ACTIVITY AREAS
- ▶ Games
- ▶ Tabletop games
- ▶ Storybooks
- ▶ Circle games

VOCABULARY

choose	guess
pretend	tell
wish	explain
remember	wonder
imagine	believe

WHAT TO DO

The words in the box are much harder to understand than the Stage Two words and also harder to teach. You may have to teach them in lots of different ways on several different occasions.

- Choose not more than one or two words at a time.

- Choose one of the activities suggested below, or plan your own activity by adapting one of them.

- Work your way through the vocabulary list one or two at a time.

- Examples of useful books can be found in Resources, pp261–2.

TEACHING IDEAS

1 **TEACHING TARGET: to understand *choose***

▶ **Tabletop games**

Simple game, eg Snakes and Ladders

Tell each child he can *choose* which token he wants to be, or which colour counter he will use. Then play the game. (Additional ideas: hide a token in each hand, close your fists and offer the two hands to a child to *choose*. Let the children *choose* whom they will sit next to. At free play time, let them *choose* between, say, trains or cars.)

2 **TEACHING TARGET: to understand *guess***

▶ **Tabletop games**

Four or five small containers and a counter

Hide the counter under one of the containers and ask a child to *guess* where it is. Are they right? If not, reveal the counter and hide it under another container. Let everybody have a turn. You can make it into a little contest by counting up which child guessed right most often. (Additional ideas: play 'Can You Guess Who I Am?' Tell the children, for instance, 'I help children to cross the road', 'I have long ears, whiskers and I like carrots', 'I look after sick people in hospital.')

3 **TEACHING TARGET: to understand *pretend***

▶ **Games**

None

Play a miming game. Whisper a 'pretend' to one child (for example, '*Pretend* to be asleep'). Can the others work out what he is pretending? Whisper a 'pretend' to another child and give everyone a turn at miming. (*Pretend* to be a bird, *pretend* to be eating something nasty). If the children find it hard, you may have to show them, or do the miming yourself. (Additional ideas: during extended play, talk about *pretending* the cars have had a crash, *pretending* the car is in the carwash.)

4 **TEACHING TARGET: to understand *tell***

▶ **Games**

None

Play Chinese Whispers. The child must *tell* his next-door neighbour what the message is, and the next child must *tell* his neighbour, and so on round the group. (Additional idea: play a 'Tell Me' game – ask the children in turn '*Tell* me what day it is. *Tell* me your name. *Tell* me what you had in your lunchbox. *Tell* me how old you are.' Later on, make it more interesting by challenging them to answer quickly.)

5 **TEACHING TARGET: to understand *wish***

▶ **Games**

None

Play a game of 'I Wish'. Start off by saying a wish of your own. It's helpful if you can explain why that is your wish (for example, 'My car is really old and rattly. I *wish* I had a lovely shiny new one' or 'I've got really straight hair. I *wish* I had curly hair.') Ask the children to tell you a *wish* of their own. (Additional idea: Read the story of Cinderella and her *wish* to go to the ball.)

6 **TEACHING TARGET: to understand *explain***

▶ **Tabletop games**

A pack of *What's Wrong?* cards (Resources, p263)

Put the pack face down on the table. The children take turns to pick up a card and look at it. Each time you say, 'Can you *explain* what's wrong with that picture?' and the child tries to give an explanation. Help as necessary. In the last resort say 'I'll explain' and do so. Examples of the pictures: dipping a paintbrush in the orange juice; a boy putting his shirt on as trousers. (Additional idea: pretend you don't know anything! Ask the children to *explain* to you how to do some very simple things – sharpen a pencil, get a drink of water, put on your coat. You may have to give them the objects to help them explain.)

7 **TEACHING TARGET: to understand *remember***

▶ **Tabletop games**

 Eight small objects and a cloth

Play a version of Kim's Game (Resources, p222). Place the objects on the table. Tell the children they have to try to *remember* all the objects they can see. Then cover the objects with the cloth. Make a note of everything the children can remember between them. At the end say, 'We *remembered* six out of eight. Now let's have another look and see what we didn't *remember*.' The next time you play, if the children were reasonably successful, increase the number of objects.

Additional idea: at the beginning of the morning tell the children you are going to give them a magic word to *remember*. At dinnertime you will ask who can *remember* it. Everyone who *remembers* will get a sticker or a smiley face. This is a longer term remembering task.

8 **TEACHING TARGET: to understand *wonder***

▶ **Circle games**

 None

A game for three or more children. Tell each child something you are wondering about, eg 'I *wonder* what is in your lunchbox? I *wonder* what you like watching on TV? I *wonder* what colour your pyjamas/nightdress are/is?' When the children have answered the questions they can think up their own.

9 **TEACHING TARGET: to understand *imagine***

▶ **Games**

 None

Give each child one or more little scenarios. Say '*Imagine* you are in a railway station/by a busy road/at an airport/in a field/in a playground – what can you hear?' Or '*Imagine* you are up in an aeroplane/under the sea in a submarine/in a dark cupboard/at a swimming pool – what can you see?' Encourage as much imagination as possible.

Additional idea: tell the children, '*Imagine* you suddenly see a witch/wizard/fairy/dragon/monster – what does it look like?' You might follow this up by getting the children to draw their imaginary figure or animal.

⑩ TEACHING TARGET: to understand *believe*

▶ **Tabletop games**

 Two miniature figures, two small boxes, a counter

Play the Betty and Ben game. Tell the child you are going to make the dolls act a little play. Keeping Betty out of the way, make Ben walk up to one of the boxes and put the counter in it. Make him walk out of sight. Make Betty come in. Make her take the counter out of its box, put it in the other one and walk away. Make Ben return to collect his counter. Ask the child, 'Where will Ben look for his counter?' 'Where does he *believe* it is?' 'Why does he *believe* it is there?' Complete the scenario by making Ben look in the original box, and display surprise and dismay.

Additional idea: ask the children a mixture of sensible and absurd questions. 'Do you *believe* there is such a thing as a unicorn? Do you *believe* there is a fish made of chocolate? Do you *believe* people can live to a hundred years old? Do you *believe* that cars can go without petrol? Do you *believe* in fairies?' Discuss their beliefs.

UNDERSTANDING ACTION WORDS
STAGE FOUR

ACTIVITY AREAS
- ▶ Small toy play
- ▶ Construction & craft
- ▶ Games
- ▶ Tabletop games
- ▶ Pencil & paper

VOCABULARY

compare	contrast
arrange	change
estimate	check
continue	describe
shade	record
identify	repeat

WHAT TO DO

The vocabulary in the box is really quite difficult, but is essential for the curriculum.

- Choose one or two words that are suitable to teach together, eg arrange/change.

- Choose one of the activities suggested below, or plan your own activity by adapting one of them.

- Work your way through the words. You may have to teach them in several different ways on several different occasions.

- Examples of useful books can be found in Resources, pp261–2.

TEACHING IDEAS

1 **TEACHING TARGET: to understand *compare***

▶ **What's the Difference? game**

 A set of *What's Different?* cards (Resources, p263)

Give a pair of cards to each child, and ask them to c*ompare* the pictures. Who can find the most differences? Keep a score.

2 **TEACHING TARGET: to understand *arrange, change***

▶ **Small toy play**

 Toy/farm animals or zoo animals

Extended play. Tell the children you are going to close your eyes while they *arrange* the animals however they like. Explain that this means putting them wherever they want. Give them a minute or two, then open your eyes. Now say you are going to close your eyes again and they have got to *change* all the animals around. When you look again, try to remember what *changes* they have made. Can they correct you?

3 **TEACHING TARGET: to understand *contrast***

▶ **Tabletop games**

 A set of *Early Opposites* cards (Resources, p263)

The children can work in pairs or on their own. If in pairs, give each child one of two contrasting pictures (clean shoes, dirty shoes). Tell the children to *contrast* their pictures. Demonstrate with a pair yourself, spelling out the contrast aloud – eg 'This box is open, this one is closed.'

4 **TEACHING TARGET: to understand *estimate, check***

▶ **Construction & craft**

 Playdough and a pair of scales

Get the children to make some balls with the playdough, as nearly as they can all the same size. When they have finished, give one child two playdough balls, one in each hand, and ask him to es*timate* which one is heavier. Explain that *estimating* is a bit like guessing, but you use your eyes, ears, hands and any known facts to help in the guessing. When the child has made his estimate, get him to *check* it by weighing the balls. Give the other children a turn.

⑤ TEACHING TARGET: to understand *continue*

▶ **Games**

None

Tell the children you are going to make up a story together. You will start it off and then in turn they will *continue* it – that means going on with the story. Begin with any simple introductory idea ('Once upon a time a boy got on the bus to go to school but …'). Ask the first child to *continue* the story and so on round the group. If you are working with only one child, take turns with him to make another contribution. If you can tape record the story, it makes a useful basis for all sorts of further language work.

⑥ TEACHING TARGET: to understand *describe*

▶ **Small toy play**

A collection of everyday things – pencil, book, apple, cup, ball

Tell the children they have to *describe* the objects – that means saying everything they can think of about them. Choose one of the objects, for example the apple. Hold it in your hand and say, 'It's round.' Pass it on to the first child and tell him to say something else about it, and so on round the group. Anyone who says the name of the object is out. How long can you keep it going? When the ideas run out, say 'You *described* that really well. Now let's see if we can *describe* this one.'

⑦ TEACHING TARGET: to understand *shade*

▶ **Pencil & paper**

Photocopy Activity Sheet 15, p256, one for each child and one for you, each sheet having five rows of shapes (square, circle, triangle, star, heart)

Tell the children to watch you – you are going to *shade* in the first shape in the first row. Shade this one from top right to bottom left. Tell the children to *shade* in their first shape exactly like yours. Continue across the first row in this way, with the children copying you. Some of the shading should be top right to bottom left, and some top left to bottom right. Now tell the children to *shade* in the remaining shapes however they like. Talk about how the lines can go different ways and how *shading* can be dark or light. When they have finished, let them compare their papers. You may want or need to explain the other meaning of 'shade', ie the shade from the sun under a tree.

8 **TEACHING TARGET: to understand** *record*

▶ **Pencil & paper**

A piece of paper with the names of participants written across the top and questions down the side

	DANNY	LISA	JARED
How many brothers?			
How many sisters?			
Which pets?			
Shoe size?			

Lead a discussion, asking the children the various questions in turn and noting down the answers. Encourage plenty of chat, for example, are the brothers older or younger, what sort of pets? At the end of the session, ask how much they can all remember about what the others told them. What sort of pet did Jared have, for example. Say 'Luckily, I *recorded* what you said.' Use the record to recap everyone's answers.

9 **TEACHING TARGET: to understand** *identify*

▶ **Tabletop games**

Sheets of Odd One Out pictures (eg *car, train, boot, bike*)

Most classrooms have odd-one-out worksheets. Give a sheet to the first child, point to the first row, and ask the child to find the odd one out. When he has done so, say 'Well done, you picked out the odd one, the one that was different. You *identified* it.' Pass the sheet to the next child, indicating the second line and saying, 'Now you *identify* the next odd one.' Continue until everyone has had a turn, using the terms *pick out* and *identify* interchangeably.

10 **TEACHING TARGET: to understand** *repeat*

▶ **Games**

None

Tell the children that parrots are birds who sometimes learn to *repeat* what people say to them. You are going to find out which of them would be the best parrot. Choose a child to be first. Tell him that he is to *repeat* exactly what you say. You will say longer and longer sentences until the parrot can't manage to *repeat* them. Then it will be someone else's turn. Keep a note of the length of sentence each parrot can manage. (Examples: 'I am a parrot.' 'I am a beautiful parrot.' 'I am a beautiful blue parrot.' 'I am a beautiful blue and red parrot.' 'I am a beautiful blue, red and yellow parrot.')

UNDERSTANDING DESCRIBING WORDS
STAGE ONE

ACTIVITY AREAS ▶

▶ Sand & Water
▶ Dressing up
▶ Hall/PE

▶ Playmat & Cars
▶ Home Corner
▶ Games

VOCABULARY

big/little	long/short
heavy	soft/hard
wet/dry	noisy
slow/fast	broken
open/shut	

WHAT TO DO

It is not practical to list all the possible adjectives a child might encounter in everyday life. Much depends on environment, culture, experience, etc.

- The lists have been arranged in the order one would expect most children to learn to understand the words we use to describe shape, size, quantity, appearance, condition, touch and sound.

- Teaching ideas are given for a selection of the most common English adjectives at Developmental Stages One, Two, Three and Four. There will be lots of other describing words which do not appear in any of the lists. Once you have made sure the child understands most of the words on the lists, you can pick any activity you think is appropriate to teach additional words.

- Examples of useful books can be found in Resources, pp261–2.

TEACHING IDEAS

1 TEACHING TARGET: to understand *big/little*

▶ **Sandtray**

Big and little buckets and spades

Parallel play. Play alongside the child, using the target words to comment on what he is doing. Make some different sized sandcastles. Comment as you make them, for example, 'You made a *big* castle. My castle is a *little* one. Here is the *little* bucket.'

▶ **Dressing up**

Big and little hats and shoes or boots

Parallel play. Let the child try the clothes on, and comment on what he is doing: 'You put the *big* hat on. This is a *little* hat, it's too *little* for me. I need a *big* hat. You need the *little* shoes.'

2 TEACHING TARGET: to understand *slow/fast*

▶ **Hall/PE**

None

Demonstrate the meaning of the words first by moving slowly, then fast. Tell the child you are going to do *slow* walking, then *fast* walking. Encourage the child to join in with you. Then give a short instruction with the target words. You might give a signal, such as clapping your hands, to gain the child's attention. Example: '*Slow* walking … *Fast* walking … *Slow* crawling … *Fast* crawling.'

▶ **Playmat**

Toy vehicles

Parallel play with the cars on the playmat. Comment on the speed as follows: 'That car goes *fast*. This old lorry is very *slow*. I'm making my car go *fast*. Your car is going very *fast*.'

3 **TEACHING TARGET: to understand *open/shut***

▶ **Home Corner**

A door to open and shut and some boxes with lids

Play a game of visiting the Home Corner, commenting on whether the door is *open* or *shut*. Put something in one of the boxes and close the lid. Then say, 'I wonder what is in the box, let's *open* it and see. Oh, now you *shut* the box.'

▶ **Games**

Puppets with mouths that can open and shut (can be made quite easily from a sock)

Play alongside the child with the puppets, commenting on whether their mouths are *open* or *shut*. Small children find it quite difficult to manipulate glove puppets, so you may have to do most of the opening and shutting actions. Examples of what you might say: 'Here comes the dragon. Look out, his mouth is *open*. Oh, now it's *shut*. Here comes the monster, his mouth is *shut*.'

4 **TEACHING TARGET: to understand *heavy***

▶ **Games**

A bag and some shopping items of various weights including some really heavy things

Fill up the bag and mime carrying a heavy item, saying 'I can't carry the bag, it's too *heavy*.' Then take out some of the shopping and say, 'That's better, it's not *heavy* now.' Let the child put things in the bag, commenting on whether they are heavy or not. If he tries to lift a heavy item, say 'That's *heavy*, isn't it?'

UNDERSTANDING DESCRIBING WORDS
STAGE TWO

ACTIVITY AREAS

▶ Storybooks
▶ Music
▶ Home Corner

▶ Games
▶ Construction & craft

VOCABULARY

fat/thin	huge
square/round	loud/quiet
quick	old/new

WHAT TO DO

It is not practical to list all the possible adjectives a child might encounter in everyday life. Much depends on environment, culture, experience, etc.

- The lists have been arranged into the order one would expect most children to learn to understand the words we use to describe shape, size, quantity, appearance, condition, touch and sound.

- Teaching ideas are given for a selection of the most common English adjectives at Developmental Stages One, Two, Three and Four. There will be lots of other describing words which do not appear in any of the lists. Once you have made sure the child understands most of the words on the lists, you can pick any activity you think is appropriate to teach additional words.

- Examples of useful books can be found in Resources, pp261–2.

TEACHING IDEAS

1 **TEACHING TARGET: to understand** *fat/thin*

▶ **Construction & craft**

Playdough

Make snakes and worms with the playdough, some fat, some thin. Comment on their size as you make them. 'You made a *fat* snake. My snake is *thin*. I'm going to make a *fat* one. Can you make a *thin* worm?'

▶ **Storybooks**

A story that has fat and thin characters

Look at the pictures with the child, commenting as you go, 'There's the *fat* monster. He's playing with the *thin* monster. Which is the *fat* dog? Can you find a *thin* dog?'

2 **TEACHING TARGET: to understand** *loud/quiet*

▶ **Music**

A selection of musicmakers (eg drum) and puppets

First demonstrate the meaning of the words. Bang loudly on a drum, saying 'That is a *loud* noise.' Then tap lightly on the drum, saying 'That was a *quiet* noise.' Give the child the drum and see if he can make loud and quiet noises with it. Do the same with a variety of instruments. When you think he understands the words you can incorporate them into a game. For example, use two puppets to represent *loud* and *quiet* noises. The giant puppet can be *loud*, the princess puppet can be *quiet*. Make a quick stage by crouching with the puppets behind a table. The child has to make a *loud* or *quiet* noise according to which puppet appears on the stage.

▶ **Home Corner**

Soft toys

Choose two soft toys, one to have a *loud* voice, the other a *quiet* voice. Demonstrate their voices, making a strong contrast between *loud* and *quiet*. Make up a little story, as in the following example:

> Teddy came in from the garden. He was hungry. 'I want my tea,' he said in his *loud* voice. 'It's here,' said Rabbit in his *quiet* voice. Teddy said, 'I want my tea' again in his *loud* voice. He didn't hear Rabbit because Rabbit's voice was so *quiet*.

You could try letting the child act out the parts, using a *loud* and a *quiet* voice.

❸ TEACHING TARGET: to understand *old/new*

▶ **Storybooks**

A suitable book

The Smartest Giant in Town (Resources, p262) is a delightful story by Julia Donaldson in which the giant replaces his old clothes with a set of new ones. Read the story with the child, pointing out the *old* and *new* clothes. Once he is really familiar with the story, see if he can find the page with the giant's *new* clothes and his *old* clothes.

▶ **Games**

A selection of items which are obviously new or old, eg pencils, rubbers, exercise books, clothes, toy cars, two containers

Put the items in a pile on the floor and have two bags or boxes ready, one for *new* and the other for *old.* Demonstrate the meaning of the words by showing the child a *new* rubber and an *old* rubber, emphasising the words. Sort some of the items into the boxes or bags, then tell the child to finish sorting. Ask him to fetch eg a '*new* pencil'.

❹ TEACHING TARGET: to understand *square/round*

▶ **Construction & craft**

Sheets of coloured paper, scissors, glue and some squares and circles to draw round

Show the child the shapes and tell him, 'This one is *square*, this one is *round*.' Let him sort them so that all the *square* shapes are in one pile and the *round* ones in another. Show him how to draw round the shapes with a pencil and then cut out the shape. Tell him you are going to make some monsters. You can then use the target words to give instructions: 'I need a *square* monster. Now I need a *round* monster.' The child can then cut out the shapes and stick them on a card. You can extend the activity by suggesting what shape various features are, for example, 'Let's give this one a *square* mouth. The monster has a *round* nose.'

▶ **Construction & craft**

A big sheet of paper and pencils or crayons

Draw the outline of a large house. You can then give the child instructions to add features to the house. 'Draw a *square* door. Draw two *round* windows and two *square* windows. The door has a *round* door knocker. There is a *square* chimney on top of the roof.' Help as necessary.

UNDERSTANDING DESCRIBING WORDS
STAGE THREE

ACTIVITY AREAS

▶ Games
▶ Tabletop games
▶ Picture books

▶ Hall/PE
▶ Construction & craft

VOCABULARY

enormous/tiny	metal/wooden
short/long	bent
curved	flat
steep	smooth/rough
shiny	dull

WHAT TO DO

It is not practical to list all the possible adjectives a child might encounter in everyday life. Much depends on factors such as environment, culture and experience.

- The lists have been arranged into the order one would expect most children to learn to understand the words we use to describe shape, size, quantity, appearance, time, condition, touch, sound, taste and smell.

- Teaching ideas are given for a selection of the most common English adjectives at Developmental Stages One, Two, Three and Four. There will be lots of other describing words which do not appear in any of the lists. Once you have made sure the child understands most of the words on the lists, you can pick any activity you think is appropriate to teach additional words.

- Examples of useful books can be found in Resources, pp261–2.

TEACHING IDEAS

1 **TEACHING TARGET: to understand *rough/smooth***

▶ **Games**

Rough and smooth objects, eg marbles, pebbles, mug, hardback book, sandpaper, nail file, piece of tree bark, piece of sacking, a cloth bag

Put the objects in a feely bag. Keep one rough and one smooth object on the table. Demonstrate the meaning of *rough* and *smooth* by going round the classroom or playground touching different surfaces so that the child can link the word to the texture. Then let him put his hand in the bag and select an object. Tell him to put it with the *rough* or *smooth* object on the table.

▶ **Tabletop games**

Four rough and four smooth textures, stuck on cards, three of each card so that altogether you have 12 cards

Lay the cards face down on the table. Demonstrate the meaning of the words by finding things that are *rough* and *smooth*. Then take turns to choose two cards. If they both have the same kind of texture they count as a pair.

2 **TEACHING TARGET: to understand *enormous/tiny***

▶ **Picture books**

A book with enormous and tiny creatures or objects

Books about animals are suitable and this may fit in with topic work, for example, about the rainforest. Go through the book with the child, pointing out some *enormous* animals or plants, and some *tiny* ones. Open the book at random and see if the child can find something *enormous* and something *tiny* on the page. Make a display of *enormous* and *tiny* animals and plants.

▶ **Hall/PE**

None

Tell the child he is on an adventure in a forest. He must listen to what you say and act accordingly. Demonstrate the meaning of the words before you start by taking an *enormous* step followed by a *tiny* step, saying the words as you do the actions. Then make up a forest adventure story, for example: 'You are walking through the forest and you come to a big puddle. Take an *enormous* step so you don't get your feet wet. Oh dear, now there is an *enormous* log in your way. You will have to climb over it. On the path you see a *tiny* key. Pick it up. It could only fit in a *tiny* door. Look, here is a tree stump with a *tiny* door in it. See if the *tiny* key fits.'

3 **TEACHING TARGET: to understand *short/long***

▶ **Construction & craft**

Playdough

Make snakes or worms out of playdough. Use the target words to talk about them: 'You're making a very *long* snake. Can you make a *short* one?' Once the child has shown some understanding of the words, direct him to make either a *short* or a *long* snake or worm.

▶ **Construction & craft**

Paper and pencils

Draw some face outlines on a large sheet of paper. Let the child put on the eyes, nose and mouth. Then talk about what sort of hair the faces should have, *long* or *short*. Tell him which face needs *long* hair and which needs *short* hair. If he gets the word meanings muddled, show him some children with *long* or *short* hair.

4 **TEACHING TARGET: to understand *metal/wooden***

▶ **Games**

Pairs of objects identical apart from the material

Present the child with two of the objects, eg a *metal* and a *wooden* spoon. Tell him what each one is made of and let him touch them, pointing out the differences in appearance and feel. Put them down on the table and ask him to point to the *wooden* spoon, then the *metal* spoon. If this is successful, give him one of the spoons and ask him to go and find something else in the room that is *metal/wooden*.

▶ **Games**

Assortment of metal and wooden objects, two empty boxes or hoops

Put the objects in a pile on the table or floor. Place two empty boxes or hoops nearby and tell the child he must sort out the big pile into *metal* and *wooden* things and put them in a box or hoop. If he does not sort the objects correctly he will need to be reminded which is metal and which is wooden, as in the above activity.

UNDERSTANDING DESCRIBING WORDS
STAGE FOUR

ACTIVITY AREAS

- ► Small toy play
- ► Hall/PE
- ► Tabletop games
- ► Circle games
- ► Pencil & paper

VOCABULARY

shallow/deep	left/right
wide/narrow	tall
silent	high/low
solid	liquid

WHAT TO DO

It is not practical to list all the possible adjectives a child might encounter in everyday life. Much depends on factors such as environment, culture and experience.

- The lists have been arranged into the order one would expect most children to learn to understand the words we use to describe shape, size, quantity, appearance, condition, touch, sound, taste and smell.

- Teaching ideas are given for a selection of the most common English adjectives at Developmental Stages One, Two, Three and Four. There will be lots of other describing words which do not appear in any of the lists. Once you have made sure the child understands most of the words on the lists, you can pick any activity you think is appropriate to teach additional words.

- Examples of useful books can be found in Resources, pp261–2.

TEACHING IDEAS

1 **TEACHING TARGET: to understand** *shallow/deep*

▶ **Small toy play**

Two water containers, some little figures (eg Lego people)

Put a small amount of water in one container and fill the other one. Pretend with the child that they are swimming pools and the Lego people are going for a swim. Explain that one of the Lego people cannot swim so he cannot go in this container 'because it is too *deep*'. Place the figure in the shallow container and say, 'This is better, this is the *shallow* pool'. Give the child instructions to place the figures in either the *deep* pool or the *shallow* pool.

▶ **Hall/PE**

None

This is an activity for a small group. Tell the children that they are in a jungle and have to keep crossing the river to keep out of danger. Show them how to walk through very deep water by holding up your arms and taking big, slow strides. Then demonstrate shallow water. Now begin a simple commentary, as in this example. 'You are walking beside the river. You can hear a tiger in the bushes! Oh dear, you must cross the river straight away! Careful, it is very *deep* just here! Phew, safe on the other side. Oh, look out, there's a stream across the path. It's OK, it's very *shallow*. How far up your shoes did the water go? Time to cross the river again, this bit looks easier if you step on those big flat stones where it is *shallow*. Whoops, you didn't see that *deep* bit, careful how you go!'

2 **TEACHING TARGET: to understand** *wide/narrow*

▶ **Pencil & paper**

A large sheet of paper

Draw a selection of wide and narrow things. For example, roads, trousers, entrances to a cave, gateways, rivers, bridges. Demonstrate the meaning of *wide* and *narrow* with real objects if you can. You could line up some chairs with a *narrow* gap between two and a *wide* gap between two others. Return to the sheet of paper and give the child instructions to put a counter on: 'A man with *narrow* trousers. A *wide* river. A *wide* cave entrance. A *narrow* gateway.'

▶ Hall/PE

None

Explain to the children that they must move around the room until you clap your hands. You will then tell them what sort of shape to make with their bodies, either *wide* or *narrow*. Extend the activity by getting them to mime as follows: going across a *wide* river, going through a *narrow* doorway.

❸ TEACHING TARGET: to understand *high/low*

▶ Hall/PE

None

You can do a similar activity to the *wide/narrow* game described above. This time the children must make a *high* or *low* shape.

▶ Tabletop game – The Owl Game

Photocopy the Race Board and the Owl Game (Resources, Activity Sheets 1 and 2, pp233–6) onto card and cut them out. You will need counters and a die.

A child throws the dice and moves his counter that number of spaces. If the child lands on a star he takes a card from the pile which tells him to put a bird on a high or low branch. If he lands on a sad face he moves back a space, if on a happy face he moves forward a space.

❹ TEACHING TARGET: to understand *left/right*

▶ Circle games

Small blank stickers, music player

To start with put a sticker on each child's right and left arm, marked R and L. Practise responding to *right/left* instructions, for example, 'Wave your *right* hand, shake your *left* leg, touch your *right* ear.' When you think the child/group is fairly confident at this level, you can play the following game. Choose an object to pass round the group. Play some music. When the music stops the child holding the object must pass it to the *right* or *left* according to your instructions.

▶ Hall/PE – Robot game

None

This can be played anywhere providing there is enough space to move backwards, forwards and sideways. Tell the children they are robots and you are their controller. Number them one and two alternately. Give instructions to move, using the target words, for example, 'Number ones, move two steps to the *right*. Number twos, move two steps to the *left*. Number ones, one step *left*, three steps *right* ' and so on.

UNDERSTANDING POSITION WORDS
STAGE ONE

ACTIVITY AREAS
- ▶ Home Corner
- ▶ Sand & water
- ▶ Hall/PE
- ▶ Songs & rhymes

VOCABULARY

up	down
in	on
off	by
inside	over
to	under

WHAT TO DO

Choose not more than two words from your target list.

- Plan activities based on the suggestions below. Remember that you may often have to teach understanding of the words in several different ways by varying the activities.

- The word lists show some of the words a child needs to understand at each stage. Your target words may or may not be included in these lists.

- Examples of useful books can be found in Resources, pp261–2.

TEACHING IDEAS

1 **TEACHING TARGET: to understand *in, on, under***

▶ **Home Corner**

 Toy furniture, teddies, dolls

Parallel play alongside the child, using the target words in short sentences, for example, 'You're putting teddy *on* the chair. I'm putting dolly *under* the table.'

▶ **Sand & water**

 Sandtray and watertray

Parallel play alongside the child, using the target words in short sentences, for example, 'You put the spade *in* the bucket. I'm pushing the bucket *under* the water.'

2 **TEACHING TARGET: to understand *over, under***

▶ **Hall/PE**

 A skipping rope between two chairs, about half a metre high

Use the target words in a short sentence while you help the child step *over* the rope or crawl *under* the rope. For example, 'You are going *over* the rope. Now you are going *under* the rope.'

▶ **Home Corner**

 Dolls, soft toys and pretend obstacles, eg a wall and bridge

Parallel play alongside the child, using the target words in short sentences, for example, 'Teddy is going *over* the wall. Rabbit is going *under* it.'

3 **TEACHING TARGET: to understand *up, down***

▶ **Songs & rhymes**

 None

Sing 'Incy Wincy Spider', emphasising *up* the spout and *down* came the rain. Remember to sing the rhyme slowly and repeat lots of times (Resources, p225).

▶ **Sand & water**

 Small vehicles

Make a big hill out of sand with the child. Drive a vehicle up the hill, saying 'My car is going *up* the hill. Now it's going *down*.' Use similar sentences as the child plays with the vehicles so that he starts to link the position word with the action.

UNDERSTANDING POSITION WORDS
STAGE TWO

ACTIVITY AREAS ▶

▶ Hall/PE
▶ Playmat
▶ Small toy play

VOCABULARY

around/round	away
behind/in front of	near
next to	outside/inside

WHAT TO DO

Choose not more than two words from your target list.

- Plan activities based on the suggestions below. Remember that you may often have to teach understanding of the words in several different ways by varying the activities.

- The word lists show some of the words a child needs to understand at each stage. Your target words may or may not be included in these lists.

- Examples of useful books can be found in Resources, pp261–2.

TEACHING IDEAS

1 **TEACHING TARGET: to understand** *behind/in front of*

▶ **Small toy play**

Animals, fields, buildings

Extended play alongside the child, suggesting ideas that involve the target words, eg 'Put the cow *in front of* the barn, put the farmer *behind* the tractor.'

▶ **Hall/PE**

A chair for each child

Demonstrate the meaning of the words by asking children to stand either *behind* or *in front of* each other. Point this out to the child who is learning the word, then ask him to stand *behind* or *in front of* someone. Repeat the activity several times. Then put out a row of chairs. Explain to the children that you will say 'Three, two, one – stand *behind* a chair!' They must all move to the right position. Repeat with *in front of*.

2 **TEACHING TARGET: to understand** *round/around*

▶ **Small toy play**

Vehicles, trees, playmat

Set out the playmat with vehicles and trees. Play alongside the child, introducing ideas involving the target words, eg 'Let's put some trees *round* the pond. Shall we drive the car *around* the house?'

▶ **Hall/PE**

Hoops and beanbags placed on the floor fairly far apart

Demonstrate the meaning of the word by choosing a child and saying, 'I'm going to walk *round* Nadim.' Group the children into pairs. Label them 'one' or 'two' and tell the 'ones' to walk *round* the 'twos'. Now give individual instructions to walk *round* either a hoop or a beanbag.

③ TEACHING TARGET: to understand *outside/inside*

▶ **Small toy play**

 Toy people, doll's house

Set up the doll's house including toy people. Encourage play involving putting some dolls *inside* the house and some *outside,* eg 'The mother wants to go *outside* – she's going *outside* for a walk.'

▶ **Farm**

 A field and a barn that animals can be put inside

Demonstrate the target words by placing an animal *inside* or *outside* a field or the barn, saying eg 'The pig is *inside* the barn.' Then give short instructions to the child to place animals in the right positions. Ask him to point out specific animals, eg 'Which cows are *inside* the field?'

UNDERSTANDING POSITION WORDS
STAGE THREE

ACTIVITY AREAS
► Small toy play
► Hall/PE

VOCABULARY

back	backwards/forwards
beside	between
high/low	middle
side	together
towards	

WHAT TO DO

Choose not more than two words from your target list.

- Plan activities based on the suggestions below. Remember that you may often have to teach understanding of the words in several different ways by varying the activities.

- The word lists show some of the words a child needs to understand at each stage. Your target words may or may not be included in these lists.

- Examples of useful books can be found in Resources, pp261–2.

TEACHING IDEAS

1 **TEACHING TARGET: to understand *backwards/forwards***

▶ **Small toy play**

Vehicles, garage

Set up the garage and vehicles. Play alongside the child, using the target words, eg 'Make the car go *backwards*. Make the van go *forwards.*'

▶ **Hall/PE**

None

The target words can be taught one to one or in a small group. Demonstrate the words by stepping either *forwards* or *backwards* as you say what you are doing. Then give instructions to move *forwards* or *backwards*. This could be single steps, hops, crawling or jumping. Do not encourage children to walk backwards because this could become dangerous.

2 **TEACHING TARGET: to understand *beside, between***

▶ **Small toy play**

Animals, fields, buildings

Extended play alongside the child, using the target words, eg 'Put the cow *beside* the sheep. Make the man stand *between* the horse and the pig.'

▶ **Hall/PE**

Mats, beanbags and hoops

The target words can be taught one to one or in a small group. Demonstrate the words by standing either *beside* or *between* the objects on the floor, describing where you are as you do it. Then give instructions to the child using the target words. If you have a small group you can make it into a game. Tell them when you blow the whistle they must get in position. Use commands such as 'Sit *beside* a hoop', 'Stand *between* a beanbag and a mat.'

❸ TEACHING TARGET: to understand *together, towards*

▶ **Small toy play**

Vehicles, playmat with town layout

Put some vehicles on the playmat. Play alongside the child using the target words, eg 'Put the van and the lorry *together*. Make the fire engine drive *towards* the supermarket.'

▶ **Hall/PE**

None

You will probably be working with a group of children. Choose two confident children to demonstrate each word meaning as you use it in a sentence. Ask them to stand in front of the rest of the group. Tell them to walk *together*. Then tell them to stop, and ask one of them to do an action, eg jump up and down. Then tell them to jump up and down *together.* Next give them short instructions to walk *towards* different parts of the room, or *towards* different people. You can then start to give instructions containing the target words to the whole group. It is best if they work in pairs because there will be plenty of options for doing things *togther* or not, and for moving *towards* various objects or people.

UNDERSTANDING POSITION WORDS
STAGE FOUR

ACTIVITY AREAS ▶

▶ Pencil & paper
▶ Small toy play
▶ Hall/PE

VOCABULARY

above/below	across
through	underneath
along	opposite
facing	against
apart	sideways
upright	

WHAT TO DO

Choose not more than two words from your target list.

- Plan activities based on the suggestions below. Remember that you may often have to teach understanding of the words in several different ways by varying the activities.

- The word lists show some of the words a child needs to understand at each stage. Your target words may or may not be included in these lists.

- Examples of useful books can be found in Resources, pp261–2.

TEACHING IDEAS

❶ TEACHING TARGET: to understand *above/below*

▶ **Pencil & paper (1)**

Paper and pencils

Give the child pencils and a sheet of paper. Tell him to draw a large square. Then ask him to put his finger *above* the square. If he does not place it correctly, show him. Then ask him to draw a cross *above* the square. Next ask him to put his finger *below* the square. Continue as for *above*.

▶ **Pencil & paper (2)**

A large sheet of paper with a thick horizontal line across the middle, counters or little bricks

Give short instructions to put the counters or bricks *above* or *below* the line. When there are three or four in each position you can ask questions such as 'Which red counters are *below* the line?'

❷ TEACHING TARGET: to understand *opposite*

▶ **Small toy play**

Small figures, eg Lego or Playmobil

Stand the figures in a group, making sure some are obviously *opposite* each other. Comment on this. 'Look, the girl is standing *opposite* the dad.' Then ask the child to rearrange the group, using the target word *opposite*. If he does not understand, demonstrate in a real life situation. For example, point out two children who are sitting *opposite* each other.

▶ **Small toys play**

A very simple 2 × 6 vertical grid drawn on a large sheet of paper (Resources, Activity Sheet 13, p254)

Place an object on each square in the top row. Then give short instructions to put a different object in the bottom row. For example, 'Put a cat *opposite* the rubber.' When all the squares have an object in them, ask questions such as 'What is *opposite* the little brick?'

③ TEACHING TARGET: to understand *sideways*

▶ **Hall/PE**

None

First demonstrate the word. Make sure all the children are looking at you, and tell them to watch carefully. Take a step to one side. This needs to be quite exaggerated at this stage. Say 'I'm stepping *sideways*.' Show them again, moving to the other side and repeating the sentence. Then give short instructions to the group that include a '*sideways*' sentence. For example, 'Take two steps forwards. Take one step back. Step *sideways*.' Vary the way they move, eg jumping, hopping, crawling and running.

▶ **Small toy play**

Toy vehicles, animals

Make an animal or vehicle move *sideways*. Comment on this, 'The car is going *sideways*.' Encourage the child to move other animals or objects *sideways*. Help him if he doesn't understand. If necessary teach him in a real life situation by standing up and stepping *sideways* while using the target word.

UNDERSTANDING COLOURS
STAGE TWO

ACTIVITY AREAS
- Small toy play
- Construction & craft
- Storybooks
- Table top games
- Pencil & paper

VOCABULARY

red	blue	green
black	white	yellow

WHAT TO DO

First make sure the child can *match* colours. If not, start with matching activities using ideas from the examples below.

- When he can match confidently, move on to teaching *one colour at a time* over several days or weeks if necessary, using ideas from the examples.

- Move on to activities involving two or more colours.

- Examples of useful books can be found in Resources, pp261–2.

TEACHING IDEAS

❶ TEACHING TARGET: to be able to match red and blue

▶ **Small toy play**

A collection of large red and blue beads and strings for threading

Put a red bead on your string. Encourage the child to copy you with the right colour bead. Carry on with reds and blues in random order until you both have a matching necklace. Lay them out side by side to compare. If the child is extremely confused about colours, avoid using the colour names just yet. Say 'Find one like this' or 'One of these' instead.

❷ TEACHING TARGET: to be able to match red, blue, green, white, yellow

▶ **Tabletop games**

Commercial colour matching game such as Match a Balloon (Resources, p263)

It may be best simply to encourage the child to place the correct colour on its matching shape at first, before you use the die to play the game properly.

❸ TEACHING TARGET: to be able to link colour name to colour (red)

▶ **Small toy play**

Small cars and other vehicles, a big piece of paper and some painting equipment

Help the child paint the paper red, and use the colour name often. Draw some 'parking spaces' on it. Now pass the vehicles one by one to the child, and ask him to 'park' the red ones in the red car park (ie on the coloured paper). Make sure he rejects any of the vehicles that are not red and gives them back to you. You might say 'No, this one will have to park in the road', placing it at a distance from the 'car park'. Reinforce the idea that the *red* cars go in the *red* car park.

❹ TEACHING TARGET: to be able to recognise that a colour has many different shades and hues

▶ **Small toy play**

A large piece of paper coloured red

Send the child off round the room to find objects that match the coloured paper. Check as he brings back each object. Is he right? Is it really *red*? If you are confined to sitting at a table, you will need a collection of small toys and objects most of which are red, but some are other colours. Ask the child to put all the *red* objects on the *red* paper, helping as much as is necessary.

5 **TEACHING TARGET: to be able to recognise a colour and its name in a story**

▶ **Storybooks**

A suitable storybook, eg *The Little Blue Car* (Resources, p262)

Read a story that illustrates the colour you are working on.

6 **TEACHING TARGET: to be able to recognise a colour in different materials**

▶ **Construction & craft**

Green paper, green paint or crayons, green fabric, etc.

Make a big collage, talking about the colour *green* as you do. Encourage the child to look for other green items to add to the collage.

7 **TEACHING TARGET: to carry out an activity involving two different colours**

▶ **Pencil & paper**

Drawing of rows of balloons on strings, enough copies for everyone

Colour the first row on your own paper in random order, using the colours you have worked on – perhaps one green, one blue, another blue, a green and so on. Avoid a definite pattern. Show the child where to start on his sheet and going by your own pattern tell him, 'Colour that balloon *green*.' When he has done so, say, 'Now a *blue* one, now another *blue* one' and so on until his row is complete. Correct errors as he goes along. Then show him your pattern and see the match.

8 **TEACHING TARGET: to be sure of two or more different colours**

▶ **Small toy play**

Collection of small objects in the target colours, eg red, blue, white cars/pencils/ balls, box for each colour, marked by a coloured dot

Spread the little objects out on the table. Explain to the children that they are going to help you sort out the things by colour into the right boxes. Give the children turns, instructing 'Put a *red* thing into the *red* box', 'Something into the *blue* box', and so on until everything has been sorted.

UNDERSTANDING COLOURS
STAGE THREE

ACTIVITY AREAS

▶ Storybooks
▶ Pencil & paper
▶ Tabletop games

VOCABULARY

pink	orange	grey
brown	purple	

WHAT TO DO

Teach the target colours one at a time, using ideas from teaching targets 1–4. The examples are in order of teaching. Each colour may take days to establish.

- Introduce activities involving two or more colours at the same time, using ideas from teaching targets 5 and 6.

- Examples of useful books can be found in Resources, pp261–2.

TEACHING IDEAS

1 **TEACHING TARGET: to match the colour pink**

▶ **Pencil & paper**

 A sheet of pictures to colour or paint for each child

Colour or paint the first picture on the sheet in pink. Give the child the task of colouring or painting the rest of the pictures to match.

2 **TEACHING TARGET: to hear about the colour pink in a story**

▶ **Storybooks**

 Suitable story

Find and read a story featuring the colour pink. Point out the colour in the picture whenever it is mentioned in the story.

3 **TEACHING TARGET: to point to pink on a page showing several different colours**

▶ **Storybooks**

 Suitable picture book

Find a story about colours. Read the story, showing the pictures as you go. Ask the child to point to anything pink he can see on each page.

4 **TEACHING TARGET: to use pink in a colouring book**

▶ **Pencil & paper**

 A page from a colouring book for each child, paints or crayons

Tell the children to colour their picture using lots of different colours, but they *must* put two *pink* things in (or more if they want). When they have finished, ask them to show you where they have coloured something *pink*. Sort out confusions or errors.

5 **TEACHING TARGET: to know the names of two or more colours (eg purple/orange, pink/grey/brown)**

▶ **Tabletop games**

Two photocopies of a simple drawing of a clothed person (Activity Sheet 18, Resources, p260), colouring pencils

Play a version of the Barrier Game (Resources, p218). Start by saying, 'I'm colouring his hat *blue*'. Colour your hat and wait for the child to do the same. Now say, 'I'm doing the jumper *orange*' and so on. When both your figure and that of the child are complete, lift the screen and see if they match. If you can spot mistakes about to be made along the way, correct them before they happen. This is a case for errorless learning.

6 **TEACHING TARGET: to know all target colours, including those from Stage Two**

▶ **Tabletop games**

A simple board game, eg Snakes and Ladders, pieces of card

Each card has one side coloured in a target colour and a number from 1 to 6 on the other. Colours and numbers do not always go together. You will need several cards, depending on the number of children playing. Spread the cards face down on the table. Instead of using the throw of a die to determine how many squares a player can move, you tell him which colour card to pick up. He looks at the number on the back and moves accordingly.

UNDERSTANDING QUESTIONS
STAGE ONE

ACTIVITY AREAS

▶ Home Corner
▶ Cooking
▶ Dressing up

▶ Games
▶ Picture books
▶ Music

QUESTIONS

What?

Which?

WHAT TO DO

If you have specific target question words in the child's IEP, choose these. If not, play alongside the child in any of the above areas, or any other relevant play opportunity.

- Use the target word as you join in the play with the child.

- Make sure the child is happy to allow you to play alongside him before you begin.

- Examples of useful books can be found in Resources, pp261–2.

TEACHING IDEAS

1 **TEACHING TARGET: to understand *Which?***

▶ **Home Corner**

 Soft toys, toy food

Parallel play alongside the child, commenting in simple phrases and sentences on what he is doing. Introduce *which?* by putting out a choice of two or three food items in front of one of the soft toys. Ask the child *which* one Teddy would like. If he does not respond, choose one for him. Repeat this at times during the activity.

▶ **Cooking**

 None

Put two or three of the cooked items on a tray and ask the child *which* one he would like. If he points to one or asks for one particular item, then he has probably understood the word *which*.

▶ **Dressing up**

 Dressing up clothes

This activity is suitable for a small group of children. Collect items that are easy to put on, such as hats, scarves, mittens. Let the children have fun putting on whatever they like to start with and describe what they are doing. 'Oh what a lovely red hat!' 'You've got the big mittens.' Put some items out on a table and let the children take turns to choose something. Prompt them by saying '*Which* hat do you want?' etc.

② TEACHING TARGET: to understand *What?*

▶ Games

Three containers (eg a box, cup and bucket), small objects

Make sure the child can point to each container when you name them, so that you know he understands what they are called. You also need some little objects that will fit easily into the containers, eg a shell, little doll, brick. Again, check the child knows what these are called. Get the child to hide his eyes or turn around while you put one object into each container. When you say 'Go!' he can look round and you ask the question '*What* is in the bucket?', etc.

▶ Picture books

Suitable book

Choose a 'lift-the-flap' type of book and first of all go through it with the child, looking under all the flaps and finding the hidden object. Once the child is familiar with the book you can ask him, '*What* is in the cupboard? *What* is under the bed?'

▶ Music

A set of sound makers

You can use musical instruments or home-made sound makers. They should all make very different sounds. Let the child play with them and enjoy making a noise. Then put them behind a barrier of some sort. Make one of the sounds and say, '*What* was that?' The child is then allowed to come and find the right sound maker.

UNDERSTANDING QUESTIONS
STAGE TWO

ACTIVITY AREAS
- ► Hall/PE
- ► Picture books
- ► Games
- ► Small toy play
- ► Home Corner
- ► Songs & rhymes

QUESTIONS

Who?

Where?

How many?

WHAT TO DO

If you have specific target question words in the child's IEP, choose these.

- If not, choose the word you want to target and plan your teaching activity based on the teaching ideas below.

- Examples of useful books can be found in Resources, pp261–2.

TEACHING IDEAS

① TEACHING TARGET: to understand *Who?*

▶ **Hall/PE**

 None

This is an activity for a small group of children. It can be done in the hall, in PE, outside or in the classroom. Make sure the child knows everyone's name. Each member of the rest of the group is given a different position to be in, for example, standing on one foot, sitting on the floor, lying on the floor, standing on a bench, etc. When everyone is in position you can ask the *who?* questions: '*Who* is standing on one foot?' '*Who* is sitting on a bench?' If the child does not respond or points to the wrong person, show him straightaway.

▶ **Picture books**

 A suitable book

Choose a picture book that includes a variety of characters on each page. First of all go through the book with the child. Use simple sentences to tell him who the characters are and what they are doing. When he is familiar with the book, choose a page and ask the *who?* questions: '*Who* is running up the hill?' '*Who* has fallen over?'

② TEACHING TARGET: to understand *Where?*

▶ **Games**

 Small objects to 'hide' and several small containers to hide them in

Make sure the child knows what the containers are called. Then tell him you are going to play a hiding game. He must shut his eyes or look away while you hide the objects. Tell him you are 'Ready!' and use the target word: '*Where* is the ball?' '*Where* is the car?'

▶ **Small toy play**

 Animals, vehicles, buildings, fields

Let the child help you set up the farm. Use the target word to get the child to show you where certain things are: '*Where* is the cow?' '*Where* is the farmer?' You can then get the child to look away while you move one of the animals or vehicles. Ask the *where?* question again.

3 TEACHING TARGET: to understand *How many?*

▶ **Home Corner**

Soft toys, toy food

Before you do this activity you must make sure the child has some idea of number and can count objects up to at least five. Set up a tea table in the Home Corner, with food items and some large soft toys. Each toy starts with an empty plate. Put some toy biscuits on the plates. Use the target question word: '*How many* biscuits has Teddy got?' '*How many* apples would Rabbit like?'

▶ **Songs & rhymes**

None

There are lots of songs and action rhymes that involve numbers, such as 'Five Little Ducks Went Swimming One Day' (Resources, p223). Choose a rhyme and teach it to the child. Sing it together, doing the actions where appropriate. Make it even more meaningful by drawing pictures or using little toys to represent the characters in the rhyme. You can then ask the target questions: '*How many* ducks went swimming?'

UNDERSTANDING QUESTIONS
STAGE THREE

ACTIVITY AREAS
- ▶ Storybooks
- ▶ Cooking
- ▶ Construction & craft
- ▶ Table top games

QUESTIONS

Why?

When?

WHAT TO DO

You may also use words from the previous stages.

- The *When?* questions involve an understanding of time words (see p110).

- Check that the child understands the time words you are using in the activities.

- You may also need to adjust the activity to use time words he does understand, eg *yesterday, today, tomorrow,* but not actual clock times.

- Examples of useful books can be found in Resources, pp261–2.

TEACHING IDEAS

1 TEACHING TARGET: to understand *Why?*

▶ **Storybooks**

A suitable book

Choose a short story with plenty of pictures. Read the story with the child, letting him look at the pictures and comment on what is happening. Ask some of the earlier, more concrete questions such as *Who? What ... doing? Where?* Once the child is familiar with the story, go through it again looking at the pictures and ask relevant *why?* questions that go with the story. When he shows you he understands the question by giving you the right answer, try shutting the book and asking some more *why?* questions.

▶ **Cooking**

A bowl, knife, selection of food

You and the child or small group are going to make a simple fruit salad. There will be lots of opportunities to ask *why?* questions as you collect the equipment and prepare the fruit. Examples include: '*Why* do we need to wash our hands?' '*Why* do we cut up the fruit?' '*Why* do we need a knife?'

▶ **Tabletop games**

A commercial set of *What's Wrong?* cards (Resources, p263), Race Board (Resources, Activity Sheet 1, p233), a die, counters

Put the cards face down beside the Race Board. When the child lands on a star he takes a card and you ask a relevant *why?* question, for example, '*Why* isn't the brush clean?' (Answer, 'She's dipping it in orange juice instead of water'). If the child has limited expressive language, accept a 'point' at the picture.

2 TEACHING TARGET: to understand *When?*

▶ **Storybooks**

A suitable book

Choose a storybook that includes times of day, days of the week or clock times, for example, *The Tiger Who Came To Tea* (Resources, p262). In this book you can ask *when?* questions as follows: '*When* did the Tiger knock at the door?' (at teatime.) '*When* did Sophie and her mum and dad go out for tea?' (in the evening/night). If the story you choose has days of the week you will have to make sure the child is familiar with the names of the days. Lots of children can recite the days of the week but cannot match a particular day to an event.

3 **TEACHING TARGET: to understand *When?***

▶ **Tabletop game – Do you know When?**

 Race Board and *When?* cards (Activity Sheets 1 and 6, Resources, p233, 242), die and counters

Copy the clues onto card and cut them out. If you land on a star you must take a card from the deck and try to answer the question. Help the child read the card if necessary. If he answers correctly he can have another throw of the die. If he makes mistakes you will have to go back a step and teach the meaning of the target words. If a player lands on a happy face he can move forward one space. If he lands on a sad face, he moves back one space.

UNDERSTANDING QUESTIONS
STAGE FOUR

ACTIVITY AREAS

- ▶ Cooking
- ▶ Games
- ▶ Reference books

QUESTIONS

How do you make?

How do you know?

WHAT TO DO

These are the most difficult type of question words and the child will need quite well developed spoken language to be able to show you that he understands the question.

- If he does not yet make sentences with words like *because, so* or *if*, it would be better to leave out this section.

- Examples of useful books can be found in Resources, pp261–2.

TEACHING IDEAS

1 **TEACHING TARGET: to understand *How do you make?***

▶ **Cooking**

 Small cards with food-related items written on them (eg sandwich, cup of tea, toast and jam, bowl of cereal, salad), or food pictures

This activity could be used as a pre-teaching session for food technology. Write *How do you make?* in large letters on the whiteboard. Read it through with the child or small group of children. Give each child a small card, placed face down in front of him. Point to the question on the whiteboard and ask the first child to turn over his small card. Help him read what it says. Then say the whole question, for example, '*How do you make a cup of tea?*' His answer will let you know if he has understood or not. His answer needs to include what you need (eg a kettle and water) and what you do (eg switch on the kettle).

▶ **Games**

 A small puppet, objects such as a greeting card, junk model, home-made book, food made from playdough

Introduce the puppet as a creature from an alien planet. Explain to the child that the puppet does not understand how to do lots of things. Let the puppet 'choose' one of the objects. The puppet then asks the child, '*How do you make playdough pizza?*' The child will show you that he has understood if he includes the following in his answer: what you have to do, what you need to have.

▶ **Reference books**

 A craft book

Choose a craft book on a subject that interests the child. Make sure it has lots of good clear illustrations. Make sure you are familiar with some of the contents before you start. Let the child have some time looking through the book. Then ask him the '*How do you make?*' question. He must find the relevant part of the book and tell you what you need and what you need to do. If he can do this, he probably understands the question.

② TEACHING TARGET: to understand *How do you know?*

▶ **Games**

Small cards with numbers 1–10 written on them

Put the cards face down on the table and let the child select three of them. He tells you which numbers he has. Remove the other cards and place the three selected ones face down. Ask the child which numbers they are. If he cannot remember, go through them again. Shuffle them round. Then you each take a card and show each other your number. Ask the child what the remaining number is. If he is correct, ask '*How do you know?*' He will show that he has understood this question by explaining why it must be that number.

▶ **Games**

Birthday Presents game (Activity Sheet 8, Resources pp246–7)

Copy the sheet showing the presents and give to the child. Go through the pictures to make sure he knows what they all are. Then read the sentences from the accompanying script sheet, one at a time. If he chooses the right item, ask the question '*How do you know?*' He will show that he has understood the question by giving you an adequate explanation. Accept any reasonable attempt at an answer.

UNDERSTANDING QUANTITY WORDS
STAGE ONE

ACTIVITY AREAS

- ► Sand & water
- ► Songs & rhymes
- ► Small toy play
- ► Construction & craft

VOCABULARY

lots	more
big bit	little bit
no more	too much
too many	

WHAT TO DO

Choose target words, not more than three or four at a time.

- Choose activity area.

- Plan activity using ideas from the examples.

- Examples of useful books can be found in Resources, pp261–2.

TEACHING IDEAS

1 **TEACHING TARGET: to understand *lots, little bit, more***

▶ **Sand & water**

Lots of different containers

Parallel play making sandcastles. Fill and empty containers, talking about having *lots* of sand or water in your bucket, or only a *little bit* so you need *more* to fill it to the brim. ('I've got *lots* of sand in my bucket. There's a *little bit* in here. Shall I put some *more* in?')

2 **TEACHING TARGET: to understand *little bit, more, too much, no more***

▶ **Sand & water**

Toy teaset

Use the teaset with the water tray to make 'cups of tea' for each other. Talk about putting a *little bit* of 'milk' in, a *little bit* more, *no more*, whoops! that was *too much*! ('I'll give you a *little bit* more milk. Here you are. Oh dear! That was *too much*! It's spilled.')

3 **TEACHING TARGET: to understand *lots, too many, no more***

▶ **Small toy play**

Cars and garage

Parallel play with cars and garage. Try getting all the cars into the garage. *Lots* will fit in, but there may be *too many* to get them all in. ('We've got *lots* of cars, haven't we? Are we going to put *lots* in the garage? Here are some *more*. There's *no more* room! So *no more* cars can go in!')

4 **TEACHING TARGET: to understand *lots, too many, no more***

▶ **Small toy play**

Farm animals, farm and playmat

Parallel play with farm animals, farm and playmat. Try making the animals walk into a field or into a barn. *Lots* will fit in, but there may be *too many*. *No more*! ('I've got lots of animals in here. That's *too many*, I can't shut the gate. I'll take one out. *No more*!')

⑤ TEACHING TARGET: to understand *little bit, big bit, more*

▶ **Construction & craft**

Playdough or modelling clay

Parallel play with playdough or modelling clay. See what you can make with a *little bit*, and what you can do with some *more*. What can you make with a really *big bit*? ('Do you want a *big bit*? Here you are. I've got a *little bit*. I need some *more*. Now I can make a big ball like yours. I can roll it to you.')

⑥ TEACHING TARGET: to understand *lots, more, too many*

▶ **Construction & craft**

Bricks, Duplo

Parallel play building towers. Start with a small supply. Talk about needing *more* to make really big towers. You may need *lots*. When the tower falls over that was perhaps *too many*. ('That's a good tower. Let's get some *more* bricks. We need *lots*. Whoops! *Too many*, it fell down. I'm going to make another one.')

⑦ TEACHING TARGET: to understand *no more*

▶ **Construction & craft**

Duplo bricks

Parallel play with Duplo bricks. Have a good supply of bricks beside you, but only put out a limited number of one colour. Help the child to make a tower or building, or make one each, saying 'Let's make something with this colour.' When you run out of bricks, say 'There are *no more* of those. We'll have to use another colour.' Get out just a few of another colour and repeat the activity, saying again when you run out, '*No more*! Let's see if I can find some more in here.'

⑧ TEACHING TARGET: to understand *more, no more, too much*

▶ **Construction & craft**

Scissors, glue, paper

Set up a cutting and glueing activity. Use the target words to help the children put on *more* glue as necessary. If they overdo it, use the words *too much* and *no more*. ('Stop, *no more*! You had *too much* glue. Let's wipe a bit off.')

UNDERSTANDING QUANTITY WORDS
STAGE TWO

ACTIVITY AREAS
- ▶ Small toy play
- ▶ Construction & craft

VOCABULARY

all of/some of	one of/two of
another	enough/more

WHAT TO DO

Choose target words (teach *all of* and *some of* before *one of* and *two of*)

- Choose activity area.

- Plan an activity using ideas from the examples.

- Examples of useful books can be found in Resources, pp261–2.

TEACHING IDEAS

1 **TEACHING TARGET: to understand *all of, another* (one)**

▶ **Construction & craft**

Duplo or Lego bricks of two different colours

This is an extended play activity. Suggest that the child make a building using *all of* the red ones, while you use *all of* the blue ones. Help sort them out, commenting when you find *another* red, or *another* blue. If the child is unsure of colour names, talk about 'another one like this' or 'another one of yours'. ('Here's *another*. And *another*. Now you've got *all of* yours. I haven't got *all of* mine. Help me find *another one* like this.')

2 **TEACHING TARGET: to understand *some of, another, enough***

▶ **Construction & craft**

Duplo, Lego

Suggest co-operating to make a house, using some of the various colours. You might use only two colours, or more. Help sort out *some of* the red ones, *some of* these ones. ('Do you think we've got *enough*? Do we need *another* one of these? *Some of* these could go on here.') As in Teaching target 1, avoid using the colour names if the child is still learning them.

3 **TEACHING TARGET: to understand *one of, two of***

▶ **Small toy play**

Animals, playmat

Extended play with animals and playmat. Suggest that the farmer wants one of all the different animals in his field. Help sort out *one of* the horses, *one of* the cows, *one of* the pigs. ('Here's *one of* the horses. Here you are, here's *one of* the cows. Can you get *one of* the pigs? Do you think the farmer would like *two of* the ducks? Here we are, one, two.')

4 TEACHING TARGET: to understand *one of, two of*

▶ **Small toy play**

 Vehicles

Extended play using lots of different vehicles. Suggest you both make a line of lorries, cars and motorbikes. Start your line, and ask the child to make one the same. Comment on what you are doing, and encourage the child to copy you. Check that he is copying you correctly. ('I'm putting *two of* the cars. Now *two of* the lorries. Now *one of* the motorbikes.') Do the lines look the same? How far do they reach? Is one longer than the other?

5 TEACHING TARGET: to understand *some of*

▶ **Construction & craft**

 Paint and brushes

Set up a painting activity, mixing colours. Have red, yellow and blue paints. Talk about making orange by mixing red and yellow. Then discover how to make green by mixing yellow and blue. ('We need *some of* this one and *some of* this one. Look what we've got now! Let's mix these ones now. We need *some of* this, and *some of* this.') If the child is still learning colour names, you can just refer to 'this one' or 'this colour'.

6 TEACHING TARGET: to understand *enough, more*

▶ **Construction & craft**

 Playdough or modelling clay

Extended play using playdough or modelling clay. Make a long worm or snake. Then give the child a little playdough, not enough to make a snake as long as yours. As he makes his snake, comment that he hasn't got *enough*. He's going to need some *more*. Give him some *more*, and see if that's *enough*. Get him to copy some other shapes – a flat pancake, a circle, a doughnut. Talk each time about whether he has got *enough* playdough to make a shape like yours. ('Your snake isn't as long as mine. You haven't got *enough*. You need some *more*. Here you are.')

7 **TEACHING TARGET: to understand *all of, some of***

▶ **Construction & craft**

Fabric scraps, coloured paper, scissors, glue and a large sheet of paper

Help the children make a collage. Decide before they start that you want them to use *all of* the material and *some of* the coloured paper, or the other way round, and adjust quantities accordingly. Comment as the collage takes shape. ('We need to use *all of* this, so can you use some more? Now what about *some of* this paper?')

8 **TEACHING TARGET: to understand *all of, one of, two of***

▶ **Construction & craft**

A sheet of paper each with a row of simple line drawings of familiar items

There need to be three of each object, in random order. Give the children some crayons. Then tell them to listen very carefully. You are going to tell them how to colour in their pictures. ('Colour *one of* the rabbits. Colour *all of* the boxes. Colour *two of* the houses' and so on.) Check on what they are doing and make sure they get it right.

UNDERSTANDING QUANTITY WORDS
STAGE THREE

ACTIVITY AREAS ▶
- ▶ Sand & water
- ▶ Construction & craft
- ▶ Pencil & paper

VOCABULARY

more than/less than	most
a few	least
fewer	same (amount)
fewest	equal (amount)
altogether	

WHAT TO DO

Choose target words.

- Teach opposites together (more than/less than, most/least, most/fewest).

- Plan activity using ideas from examples.

- Examples of useful books can be found in Resources, pp261–2.

TEACHING IDEAS

1 **TEACHING TARGET: to understand *more than, less than, most, least***

▶ **Sand & water**

 Identical transparent containers, one for each person

Extended play. Ask everyone to put some sand or water into their container, without watching what everyone else is doing. Now look at all the containers. Help the children decide who has the *most*. Who has the *least*? Line up the containers in order from *most* to *least*. Comment on who has *more than* somebody else, who has *less than* another. ('Cherry has *more than* Joshua. Ellie has *less than* Angus.')

2 **TEACHING TARGET: to understand *same* (amount), *equal* (amount)**

▶ **Sand & water**

 Identical transparent containers, one for each person

Extended play. Choose a child and say that you and he are going to see if you can put the *same* amount of sand (or water) into your containers. Keep comparing and adjusting until the amounts look *equal*. Now tell all the children to put sand or water into their containers and try to get the *same* (*equal*) amounts in all of them. Say you won't watch, but will give them a minute to do it in. Then have a look. Are the amounts the *same* or *equal*? Use the terms interchangeably.

3 **TEACHING TARGET: to understand *most, least***

▶ **Pencil & paper**

 None

Tell the story of *Goldilocks and the Three Bears* (Resources, p262) to the children and have a discussion about who had the *most* porridge, and who had the *least*, and how you can tell. Get the children to draw the three bowls for Daddy Bear, Mummy Bear and Baby Bear, a big one, a middle-sized one and a very small one, showing who had the *most* and who the *least* porridge.

④ TEACHING TARGET: to understand *a few, fewer, fewest*

▶ **Pencil & paper**

 Sheets of paper with big and small circles drawn on, counters

The smallest circles should be able to contain about three or four counters and the largest not more than six or seven. Give the children a handful of counters and tell them to put *a few* counters into all the circles, just as many as will fit. Talk about having put *a few* into the big circles, *fewer* into the next sized circles and *the fewest* into the smallest circles. Ask the children to colour the circle with the *fewest* counters in it.

⑤ TEACHING TARGET: to understand *How many?, most, fewest, altogether*

▶ **Construction & craft**

 Lego

You need to make some simple Lego constructions for each child containing different numbers of bricks but none more than about ten. Give each child a model and ask them to count *how many* bricks they need to make one like it. Hand out the required number of bricks to everybody. When they have finished, ask them all again *how many* bricks they needed. Make a note of who needed the *most* and who needed the *fewest*. Let these two compare their models. Finally, pull the models apart and put the bricks together in the middle of the table. All count them. 'How many bricks did you use *altogether*?'

⑥ TEACHING TARGET: to understand *same* (amount), *equal* (amount)

▶ **Construction & craft**

 Playdough or modelling clay, knife, ruler

Help the children flatten the playdough into a large 'cake'. If several children are playing, tell them that they are rather quarrelsome children who all want the *same amount* of cake at the party. If you are working with only one child, make it into a story about a group of quarrelsome children. Start cutting the cake, making the first two slices widely different in size. Does anyone spot it? Get the ruler out and see how different they are. Measure with the ruler. Stress that you are trying to give everyone *the same* or *equal* amounts. Carry on with the game until the children are satisfied that there are fair shares for all.

7 **TEACHING TARGET: to understand *a few, more than, fewer than, same* (equal)**

▶ **Pencil & paper**

 A bag of buttons, paper and pencil for each child, crayons

Tell the children to dip their hands into the bag and pull out *a few* buttons. Try to engineer things so that nobody has more than about six. Ask the children to draw their buttons on their piece of paper and colour them in. When they have finished, compare their collections. 'Lucy has *more than* Jo. Jo has *fewer than* Lucy and Rashid. Lucy and Rashid have the *same* (*equal*) number.' Encourage the children to talk about their buttons. 'What might this big button have come off? This one is shiny. This one is rough. This one has four holes and this one only two.'

8 **TEACHING TARGET: to understand *altogether***

▶ **Tabletop games**

 Pairs cards (Resources, p219)

Limit the number of cards you put out to a number that the children are familiar with. Join in a game of Pairs. When all the cards have been claimed, ask each child to count how many cards he has won. Then put all the cards in the middle of the table and pick them up one by one, counting as you go and encouraging the children to count in unison with you. ('There! We had 20 cards *altogether*.')

UNDERSTANDING QUANTITY WORDS
STAGE FOUR

ACTIVITY AREAS
- ▶ Construction & craft
- ▶ Tabletop games
- ▶ Pencil & paper
- ▶ Games

VOCABULARY

either/or	all except
part	every other
pair	one less
about right	roughly
exactly	exact

WHAT TO DO

Choose target words.

- Plan activity using ideas from the examples.
- Examples of useful books can be found in Resources, pp261–2.

TEACHING IDEAS

1 **TEACHING TARGET: to understand *either/or***

▶ **Tabletop games**

Snakes and Ladders, counters

Offer the child a choice. 'You can be *either* a red counter *or* a yellow counter' 'You can have *either* the dog *or* the hat.' On first introducing the concept of either/or, hold the alternatives one in each hand as you offer the choice, for example a red counter in your right hand, a yellow one in your left hand. Play the game in the usual way (Resources, p220).

2 **TEACHING TARGET: to understand *pair***

▶ **Tabletop games**

Pairs cards (Resources, p219)

Play Pairs in the usual way. Whenever a child finds two identical pictures, say 'Well done, you've found a *pair*. Two the same. You can keep the *pair*.' (On another occasion, play with the Things That Go Together cards, Resources, p263, explaining that these pairs are not exactly the same as each other. They go together because, for example, a canary lives in a cage, a hammer bangs in nails, a train runs on a track. Emphasise that a pair is always two.)

3 **TEACHING TARGET: to understand *every other***

▶ **Pencil & paper**

Photocopy the grid (Activity Sheet 14, Resources, p255), one for yourself and one for each child

you	cupcakes	are	pink	very	silly	clever	furry	children

Make up a sentence, putting a word in every other box in the first line, eg, 'You are very clever children.' Put some nonsensical words every other box, so that your sentence reads something like: 'you cupcakes are pink very silly clever furry children'. Write the words in the children's grids. Start the children off with their pencils poised over the first box. Tell them they are to put a dot on *every other* box. Demonstrate with your finger along the line of boxes. When they have finished, take one of their grids and by looking at your own read out the 'magic' hidden sentence. If the child has made a mistake, read out the nonsensical word from the box he has wrongly marked. If he has got it all right the children will hear a proper sentence. If there are any mistakes, they will hear a nonsense sentence. Repeat with another line until your imagination runs out!

4 **TEACHING TARGET: to understand *part***

▶ **Construction & craft**

Large floor puzzle

Join the children in putting the puzzle together. Talk about finding parts of the picture. ('I think I've got the *part* that goes here. Has anyone got *part* of his hat? That looks like *part* of the house.')

5 **TEACHING TARGET: to understand *all except***

▶ **Pencil & paper**

Photocopy Activity Sheet 15 (Resources, p256), one sheet for each child. On the paper are shapes in rows, lined up vertically

Tell the children to put their crayon at the beginning of the first row. Show anyone who is doubtful. Then say 'Colour all the shapes *except* the square.' Watch to see that they are getting it right and help where necessary. Tell them to move on to the next row. 'Now colour all the shapes *except* the circle.' Continue until they have completed all the rows. Compare all the sheets and see if they all have a nice straight diagonal line of uncoloured shapes.

6 **TEACHING TARGET: to understand *roughly, exactly***

▶ **Games**

Ten small objects, a large cloth

Hide some of the objects underneath the cloth. Tell the children you will lift the cloth for just a few seconds, while they look at the objects. Then replace the cloth and ask them in turn *roughly* how many things they thought they could see. Explain the word *roughly*: 'as near as you can', 'make a good guess'. Repeat several times, changing the number of objects under the cloth. If anyone guesses the right number, say 'That's *exactly* right. You guessed six and there were six.'

7 **TEACHING TARGET: to understand** *about right, roughly, exactly*

▶ **Construction & craft**

 Playdough or modelling clay, a set of scales

Divide up the playdough between the children, saying you are giving them all *roughly* the same amount. Explain that this means as nearly equal as you can guess. You are making a rough guess. Ask the children to weigh their own and their neighbour's playdough in their hands and decide if they are *roughly* the same weight. They can take bits off and stick bits on and keep weighing until they do think they are *about right*. Then take the lumps of playdough from two children who have been working together and weigh them on the scales. Were they *about right*? Help the children adjust the lumps until they are *exactly* the same.

8 **TEACHING TARGET: to understand** *one less, two less*

▶ **Games**

 None

You need at least six children for this game. Seat the children in a circle, and play the Forbidden Number game. Explain to the children that they are going to count round the circle, starting with 'one'. Choose a 'forbidden number', eg 'number three'. Tell the children that they must not say 'three', but instead say 'buzz'. Before you start, count out loud the number of children playing. Every time a child is 'out' count the children again and say, 'Only five now – that's *one less*. Only four now – that's *one less*', until only the winner is left in the game. As soon as someone is out, choose a different forbidden number and start the counting again. When the counting goes beyond ten the children should say, for example, 'twenty-buzz' for twenty-three and so on.

UNDERSTANDING SENTENCES
STAGE ONE
Three information words

ACTIVITY AREAS

- ▶ Hall/PE
- ▶ Sand & water
- ▶ Home Corner
- ▶ Games
- ▶ Small tray play
- ▶ Construction & craft

SENTENCE TYPES

ACTION–OBJECT–PERSON
Push the *car* to *Emma*.

OBJECT–PLACE–ADJECTIVE
The *key* is *under* the *big* pot.

OBJECT–POSSESSION–OBJECT
The *dog* is in *Mummy's car*.

OBJECT–PREPOSITION–PLACE
The *book* is *by* the *phone*.

PERSON–ACTION–OBJECT
Sam is *brushing* the *dog*.

WHAT TO DO

Read the section on Information Words before you start these activities (Resources, p229).

- Make sure the child understands the vocabulary you are using. If necessary you may need to teach some of the vocabulary, such as position words, before you start.

- If the child cannot carry out the command, consider reducing the number of information words.

- Examples of useful books can be found in Resources, pp261–2.

TEACHING IDEAS

1 **TEACHING TARGET: to understand sentences with Action–Object–Person**

▶ **Hall/PE (1)**

Beanbags, hoops

Use the target sentence type to give short instructions, eg '*Kick* the *beanbag* to *Joe*.' If the child does not carry out the instruction, do it yourself straightaway as you say the sentence. Then tell him to do the same action to a different person. You may need to demonstrate and check as above several times. You can vary the action words to include roll, throw, slide, eg '*Slide* the *hoop* to *Tilak*.'

▶ **Hall/PE (2)**

None

You will need a small group of children for this activity. The actions involved may be waving, shaking, pointing. Demonstrate the meaning of the sentence by doing the first action yourself – 'I'm *waving* my *hand* at *Sunita*.' Then ask the children to stand in a circle and give each an instruction, one at a time, eg '*Point* your *foot* at *Ben*. *Shake* your *head* at *Mia*.'

▶ **Sand & water**

Toy people, vehicles

Introduce the target sentences while the child is playing in the sandtray. Do the action as you say the sentence, 'I'm *pushing* the *car* to the *man*.' Then give the child instructions using the same sentence type, '*Carry* the *sand* to the *boy*. *Push* the *lorry* to *me*.'

2 **TEACHING TARGET: to understand sentences with Object–Place–Adjective**

▶ **Home Corner**

Toy crockery and cutlery the same colour and design but two different sizes, toy food

Demonstrate the target sentence, for example, 'The *banana* is *on* the *little* plate. The *orange* is *under* the *big* plate.' Remember to keep the *big/little* object the same, eg a plate. If you add another alternative you will increase the number of information words to four. Give the child instructions to arrange other food items using the target sentence type.

▶ **Games**

Two similar shopping bags or baskets, one large and one small, and a variety of shopping items

Put the baskets and shopping items on the floor. Demonstrate the target sentence. 'I'm putting the *book beside* the *big* basket.' Give the child instructions using the same sentence type, 'Put a *pencil in* the *little* basket. Put an *eraser under* the *little* basket.'

▶ **Small toy play**

Identical items of furniture apart from their size, some figures

Demonstrate the target sentence, 'The *mum* is *behind* the *big* sofa. The *girl* is *on* the *little* sofa.' Then give the child instructions using the same sentence type. Make sure you do not increase the number of information words by having too many alternatives – there should only be one *big/little* item.

③ TEACHING TARGET: to understand sentences with Object–Possession–Object

▶ **Small toy play**

Furniture, people, objects, doll's house

Talk about the various items, then demonstrate the target sentence as you carry out the action: 'The *cat* is on *granddad's chair*.' Repeat this with other objects and people. Then give the child short instructions using the target sentence. 'Put the *toys* on the *girl's bed*.'

▶ **Home Corner**

Large dolls and soft toys, crockery and cutlery and toy food

Demonstrate the target sentence as you carry out the action: 'I'm putting a *biscuit* on *Teddy's plate*.' Then give the child instructions using the same sentence type, varying the items used: 'Put a *spoon* in *Rabbit's cup*. Put an *apple* on *Dolly's plate*.'

▶ **Small toy play**

Fields, animals, tractors, people and buildings

You will need to designate fields and buildings to particular animals in order to use the target sentence. Put the cow in a field and tell the child it is 'cow's field'. Put a pig in a barn and call it 'pig's barn'. Demonstrate the meaning of the target sentence. Put a tractor in one of the animals' fields and say, 'The *tractor* is in *horse's field*.' Then give the child similar instructions.

▶ Construction & craft

Playdough

You will need a small group of children. Make some dough food such as pizzas and cakes. Then make some little things to put on them, such as cherries or olives. Each child should have a pizza and a cake and little items suitable for toppings. Demonstrate the meaning of the target sentence, eg 'I'm putting an *olive* on *Joe's pizza*. I'm putting a *cherry* on *Jade's cake*.' You can then give instructions using the same sentence type. You can make it more fun by using absurd combinations, such as olives on the cake or chocolate buttons on the pizza.

④ TEACHING TARGET: to understand sentences with Object–Preposition–Place

▶ Home Corner

Toy kitchen equipment and play food

Demonstrate the meaning of the target sentence, for example, 'I'm putting the *biscuit under* the *plate*.' Then give similar instructions to the child, varying the position words to include *in, on* and *under*.

▶ Hall/PE

Beanbags, balls, benches and mats

Demonstrate the target sentence, for example, 'The *beanbag* is *on* the *bench*. The *ball* is *under* the *mat*.' Give the child instructions using the same type of sentence.

▶ Small toy play

Fields, animals, tractors, people and buildings

Demonstrate the target sentence, for example, 'The *tractor* is *in* the *barn*. The *trailer* is *behind* the *barn*.' Then give the child instructions using the same sentence type as he plays with the toys. Make sure he understands position words such as *behind, in front of* if you want to use these words.

▶ Small toy play

People, furniture, doll's house

You can use the target sentence to instruct the child to set up the rooms in the doll's house, for example, 'Put the *chair in front of* the *table*. Put the *cupboard beside* the *sink*.' You could also play a sort of Hunt the Thimble type of game. Select two small objects to go somewhere in the house. Ask the child to look away and 'hide' each object. You then tell the child the location. 'The *book* is *under* the *bed*. The *cushion* is *behind* the *cupboard*.'

5 **TEACHING TARGET: to understand sentences with Person–Action–Object**

▶ **Home Corner**

 Soft toys, furniture

Start by using the target sentence type to describe what the child is doing, eg '*Dolly* is *sitting* on the *table*.' Repeat this sentence type with other toys, actions and objects. Then give a short instruction, eg 'Make *Rabbit wash* the *spoon*.' Repeat this sentence type with different toys and actions.

▶ **Hall/PE**

 Balls, beanbags

Use the target sentence type to give short instructions, eg '*Joe*, *kick* the *ball*. *Anna*, *throw* the *beanbag*.' If the child does not carry out the instruction, do it yourself straightaway as you say the sentence. Then tell him to do the same action to a different person. You may need to demonstrate and check as above.

▶ **Small toy play**

 People, furniture

Start by using the target sentence type to describe what the child is doing, eg 'The *girl* is *opening* the *door*.' Then make suggestions to the child, using the target sentence type, eg 'Make the *mum carry* the *chair*. Make the *dad pick up* the *baby*.'

▶ **Farm**

 Fields, animals, tractors, people and buildings

Spend a little time playing alongside the child, using the target sentence, eg 'The *man* is *pushing* the *pig*. This *horse* is *eating* the *hay*.' Then give the child short instructions: 'Make the *cow jump* in the *field*. Make the *dog chase* the *sheep*.'

UNDERSTANDING SENTENCES
STAGE TWO
Four information words

ACTIVITY AREAS
- ▶ Hall/PE
- ▶ Playing field/ playground
- ▶ Small toy play
- ▶ Construction & craft
- ▶ Games

SENTENCE TYPES

ACTION–ADJECTIVE–OBJECT–PERSON
Push the *blue car* to *Emma*.

PERSON–ACTION–ADJECTIVE–OBJECT
Make the *dog sit* on the *big rug*.

ADJECTIVE–OBJECT–PREPOSITION–PLACE
The *old dog* is *under* the *bed*.

PERSON–OBJECT–PREPOSITION–POSSESSION
Sam put the *key by Dad's* bag.

WHAT TO DO

Read the section on Information Words before you start these activities (Resources, p229).

- Make sure the child understands the vocabulary you are using.

- You must also make sure that the child can understand sentences with three information words first.

- You may need to teach some of the vocabulary, such as position words, before you start.

- If the child cannot carry out the command, consider reducing the number of information words.

- Make sure there is an alternative for each information word as in the following example: *Roll (kick)* the *big (little) hoop (ball)* to *mum (dad)*.

- The adjectives can include any relevant words, and they should correspond approximately with the Describing Words stages one and two (pp42–47).

TEACHING IDEAS

1 **TEACHING TARGET: to understand sentences with Action–Adjective–Object–Person**

▶ **Hall/PE**

Balls, beanbags of two different colours

This activity works best with three children – the child who is learning and two others. Each child stands in a space. Put the balls and beanbags in the centre. Then use the target sentence to give instructions, eg '*Roll* the *red ball* to *Sam*. *Kick* the *blue beanbag* to *Jess*. *Throw* the *blue ball* to *Jess*.'

▶ **Playing field or playground**

Some ride-on toys, tricycles or scooters in two different sizes

You need a minimum of three children. Place two of the children about 10 metres away, facing you. Put the ride-ons near the children. Use the target sentence to give the instruction, '*Ride* the *big scooter* to *Tom*. *Push* the *little tricycle* to *Mia*. *Push* the *little scooter* to *Tom*.'

2 **TEACHING TARGET: to understand sentences with Person–Action–Adjective–Object**

▶ **Small toy play**

People, furniture, doll's house

Set up the doll's house with a variety of people and furniture. There should be a difference either in sizes or colours of furniture. Talk with the child about who lives in the house and make sure he understands the vocabulary you are going to use. You can then give instructions using the target sentence as follows: 'Make the *dad stand* on the *little chair*. Make the *girl sit* on the *blue bed*. Make the *dog lie* on the *red bed*.'

▶ **Hall/PE**

Two different colours of hoops and beanbags

This is an activity for a small group of children. Place the hoops and beanbags in a straight line. Use the target sentence to tell the child where the other members of the group must stand, for example: 'Tell *Kia* to *stand in* a *green hoop*. Tell *Max* to *stand* by a *blue beanbag*. Tell *Ross* to *sit* on a *yellow beanbag*.' When the group are all in position they could run a race to the end of the hall.

3 **TEACHING TARGET: to understand sentences with Adjective–Object–Preposition–Place**

▶ **Small toy play**

Identical animals apart from size or colour, farm, vehicles

Let the child help set up the farm with fields, buildings and vehicles. You can then give instructions using the target sentence as follows: 'Put the *little sheep behind* the *barn*. Put the *big pig in front of* the *tractor*. Put the *big cow beside* the *farmer.*'

▶ **Construction & craft**

Paper, coloured pencils or felt-tip pens

You are going to use the target sentence to tell the child how to make a picture. First draw the outlines of a house and a tree on a big sheet of paper. Make sure there are some coloured pencils or crayons. You can then proceed with the instructions as follows: 'Draw a *brown rabbit under* the *tree*. Draw a *black bird on top* of the *house*. Draw a *green apple in* the *tree.*'

4 **TEACHING TARGET: to understand sentences with Person–Object–Preposition–Possession**

▶ **Small toy play**

Toys cars and lorries, two garages and four small figures such as Lego people

Two of the figures will be 'drivers' and the other two 'owners'. Give the characters names, and spend some time talking about them so that the child is familiar with the names. Set up the garages so that they are facing the child, with the 'owners' standing beside them. Use the target sentence as follows: 'Make *Sam* drive a *lorry behind Mr Jones'* garage. Make *Ali* drive a *car into Mr Smith's* garage. Make *Ali* drive a lorry *in front of Mr Jones'* garage.'

▶ **Games**

A box/bag for each child, about 12 small objects

This is an activity for a small group of children. Place the small objects in the middle of the table. Each child puts his bag or box in front of him. You are then ready to use the target sentence as follows: 'Tell *Gemma* to put a *cube in Danny's* bag. Tell *Aaron* to put a *rubber beside Tyler's* bag. Tell *Rani* to put a *pencil under Ethan's* bag.'

UNDERSTANDING SENTENCES
STAGE THREE
Following two-step instructions

ACTIVITY AREAS

▶ Games
▶ Pencil & paper
▶ Construction & craft
▶ Circle games

▶ Hall/PE
▶ Tabletop games

EXAMPLES

Fetch a book and sit on the carpet.

Stick on a circle and draw a square.

WHAT TO DO

Children with poor listening and attention skills often have great difficulty following instructions, especially those aimed at the whole class. Although they may understand all the words in the sentence, they do not process the meaning of the sentence as a whole.

- The instructions in the examples consist of two main elements. You could increase this to three if you think the child can succeed.

TEACHING IDEAS

1 **TEACHING TARGET: to be able to follow simple instructions**

▶ **Games – Simon Says (Resources, p223)**

 List of Simon Says instructions (Activity Sheet 3, Resources, p237)

A small group game. If possible you need two adults, one to give the instructions and the other to record the child's responses. If he consistently fails to follow two instructions you should adjust the game so that he only has one until he is more confident. You can teach him to follow two instructions in a one-to-one setting. At this stage give the instructions without 'Simon Says' and the children should try to follow all of them.

▶ **Construction & craft**

 Card, scissors, coloured paper, pens and pencils, glue

In this example you will be giving two-part instructions to make a greetings card. You can apply the same ideas to any other craft activity. Explain to the child that he will need to listen carefully. To start with you will repeat sentence twice and wait while the child carries out the instructions. As he gets more confident and succeeds, try only saying the instructions once. Examples: 'Fold the card in half and open it out. Write HAPPY BIRTHDAY on the right side, then close the card. Cut out a big yellow circle and stick it on the front. Cut out some petal shapes and draw a stem. Stick the petals on and draw some leaves.'

▶ **Pencil & paper**

 An exercise book, pencil, ruler, rubber and colours

This activity teaches the child to follow the kind of instructions that are given by teachers involving setting out a piece of work. You may do this as a specific teaching activity, or use the same approach in a real life situation. This example uses maths. These are the kind of instructions: 'Open your book and find the next clean page. Draw a line down the middle of the page and write Date at the top. Write the title, ADDING, and underline it. Put a number One in the margin and copy down this sum (15 + 10 =).' Each of these instructions contains two elements. You can adapt any lesson to make the same kind of instructions.

▶ **Construction & craft**

 Lego or similar construction equipment

Decide with the child what he is going to make. You could make this more fun by suggesting that you are the 'designer' and he is the 'engineer'. He has to follow your exact instructions. You then proceed to give two-part instructions as described in the following examples. 'Get a baseboard and fix red pieces along one end. Fix yellow pieces on the other end and blue on both sides. Put another row all the way round using any colours you like. Make a doorway and put in two windows.'

UNDERSTANDING SENTENCES
STAGE FOUR
Following more complex instructions

ACTIVITY AREAS
- ▶ Games
- ▶ Pencil & paper
- ▶ Construction & craft
- ▶ Circle games
- ▶ Hall/PE
- ▶ Tabletop games

EXAMPLES

Write your name before you draw a house.

Tell me a food that is round but not an orange.

WHAT TO DO

Children with poor listening and attention skills often have great difficulty following instructions, especially those aimed at the whole class. Although they may understand all the words in the sentence, they do not process the meaning of the sentence as a whole.

- Make sure the child understands the vocabulary you are using.

- If he cannot carry out the instructions demonstrate what you mean then try again.

- If he is still having difficulty he may not be ready for this level of complexity yet.

TEACHING IDEAS

1 **TEACHING TARGET: to be able to follow complex instructions**

▶ **Circle games**

None

This is a game for a small group. The children must listen for the instruction and work out whether it applies to them or not. Examples: 'If you have curly hair, sit on the floor. If you like apples, clap your hands. If you have a sister, sit down. If you have a brother, turn around.' You can personalise these kinds of instructions to involve details of where people live, what their name starts with, etc.

▶ **Hall/PE**

None

A game for a small group. Divide the group into two and call one group the cats, the other group the mice. Tell the child they must walk around the room until you clap your hands. Then everyone must stand still while you give an instruction, for example: 'If you are a mouse, run to the door. If you are a cat, catch a mouse [by gently tapping on one shoulder]. If you caught a mouse, bring it to me.'

▶ **Games – Riddle game**

Race Board and Clues Cards (Activity Sheets 1 and 4, Resources pp233, 238–40), die and counters

Copy the clues on to card and cut into separate cards. If a player lands on a star, take the top Clue card and read it to him. If he gives a plausible answer he can move forward three spaces. If not, other players can try to answer. If they are correct they move forward three spaces. The happy/sad faces mean one step forward or back.

▶ **Tabletop game – Find the family**

A coloured die, counters and Letter Cards (Activity Sheet 5, Resources p241)

Copy the letter cards on to individual cards. On a separate sheet of paper write the names of six categories: for example, food, clothes, buildings, sports, furniture, vehicles. Give each category a colour to correspond with the colours on the die. Put the letter cards in a pile face down. The first child rolls the die. You take the top card from the pile and give the following instruction, according to the colour rolled: 'Tell me a *food* that starts with *s*.' If the child answers correctly he wins a counter. Continue in the same way, encouraging the children to give new items, not ones already given. You can add to the letters if you wish.

UNDERSTANDING TIME WORDS
STAGE ONE

ACTIVITY AREAS
- ▶ Home Corner
- ▶ Sand & water
- ▶ Songs & rhymes
- ▶ Hall/PE
- ▶ Picture books
- ▶ Construction & craft

VOCABULARY

now	again
today	night (time)
soon	in a minute

WHAT TO DO

Make the Special Calendar (Activity Sheet 7, Resources, pp243–5). Many of the activities in the Time Words section use the Special Calendar.

- Choose one of the activities suggested below, or plan your own activity by adapting one of them.

- Work your way through the vocabulary one or two at a time. You will almost certainly have to teach these words in several different ways on many different occasions. Include whichever ones are being worked on in general classroom instructions.

- Examples of useful books can be found in Resources, pp261–2.

TEACHING IDEAS

1 **TEACHING TARGET: to understand *now***

▶ **Hall/PE**

 None

Hide and Seek (Resources, p221). You need at least two or three children, and to have a second adult is a great help. Get all the children except one to shut their eyes and take the last child to hide. When he is hidden, go back to the other children and tell them to open their eyes. Explain that they are going to look for Lily, who is hiding. Hold your hand up like a traffic policeman and say, 'Are you ready to look for her? Off you go NOW!' using a big voice on the word *now* and dropping your hand. Help them to hunt about. If they don't find Lily quickly, call to her to say 'Cuckoo!' loudly. When she has been found, repeat with another hider, again using the word *now* as the signal to start hunting. If children have never played this game before, a second adult is really vital, either to hold back the seekers or to stay in hiding with the hider.

2 **TEACHING TARGET: to understand *again***

▶ **Construction & craft**

 Large bricks

Parallel play. Join the child in building towers or tall houses, and either knocking them down or piling on brick after brick until they fall down of their own accord. Then say, 'I'm going to build it *again*. Are you building yours *again*?' Carry on building and knocking down in this way until the child has had enough or time runs out.

3 **TEACHING TARGET: to understand *again***

▶ **Songs & rhymes**

 None

Sing an easy song with the children, preferably one with actions (eg 'If You're Happy and You Know It (Resources, p224)). When you get to the end, say 'Let's sing it *again*.' Do so!

④ TEACHING TARGET: to understand *in a minute*

▶ **Hall/PE**

Skipping ropes

Make a large circle on the floor with rope or skipping ropes. Explain to the children that you are going to shut your eyes and they are all to get in the circle. Then you will open your eyes and see if they are all in. Shut your eyes, wait a few seconds, then say '*In a minute* I'm going to have a look.' Count to about ten under your breath, then open your eyes and see. ('Emily, you aren't in the circle! Get in! Well done everybody!') Then say you are going to shut your eyes again and everyone is to get out of the circle. Shut your eyes, say 'I'm going to look *in a minute*', count to ten and proceed as before. (Whenever you tell the children that something is going to happen *in a minute,* make sure that it really is no longer than a minute, and preferably not more than 30 seconds.)

⑤ TEACHING TARGET: to understand *today*

▶ **Construction & craft**

Special Calendar (Activity Sheet 7, Resources, pp243–5)

Use the Special Calendar at the beginning of every day. Choose a picture of something that is going to happen during the day, for example PE. Help the child attach the picture to the calendar, saying 'Look, we're going to have PE *today.* Let's stick the PE picture on.' If possible, revisit the calendar after PE has taken place, look at the calendar together and say, 'See, we did PE *today*, didn't we?'

⑥ TEACHING TARGET: to understand *night*

▶ **Picture books**

A picture book with pictures of night-time and night-time activities (moon, stars, dark, child, toys or animals going to bed)

A storybook may have good night-time pictures in it that you can use to talk about, without necessarily reading the whole story which may be above the child's language level. Talk about how it gets dark at *night*. We turn the lights on. We can sometimes see the moon and stars. We go to bed and go to sleep in the *night*. Point out the bed pictures on the Special Calendar (Activity Sheet 7, Resources, pp243–5).

7 **TEACHING TARGET: to understand** *today, night, time, night-time*

▶ **Home Corner**

Large dolls, teddies, beds

Parallel play. Join the children putting the dolls and teddies to bed, kissing them goodnight, singing them a song, then getting them up again. ('It's *night-time* now. I'm putting my teddy to bed – in you go, Teddy. Good*night*. Sleep well. I'll turn the light off.' And later :'Open the curtains. Hullo, Teddy. *Time* to get up! *Time* to get dressed! *Time* for breakfast! What shall we do *today*?'

8 **TEACHING TARGET: to understand** *soon, now*

▶ **Sand & water**

Any

Parallel play in the sandtray or watertray. About three or four minutes before it is time to stop and clear up, say '*Soon* it will be time to stop. Let's finish our castles/towers/roads.' Allow the three or four minutes to pass and then say, 'Time to stop *now*.' (*Soon* can mean a few minutes, a few hours, days or weeks, or even longer, depending on the context. For young children at this stage, *soon* must be within three or four minutes, as after that it becomes meaningless.)

UNDERSTANDING TIME WORDS
STAGE TWO

ACTIVITY AREAS ▶

▶ Construction & craft
▶ Storybooks

VOCABULARY

morning	after
afternoon	holiday
birthday	tomorrow

WHAT TO DO

Add pictures to the Special Calendar indicating mid-morning fruit/snack time, dinnertime, playtime, and hometime (Activity Sheet 7, Resources, pp243–5).

- Visit the Special Calendar with the child first thing every day.

- Choose one of the words on the vocabulary list or a small group of words that can conveniently be taught together, as in Teaching Target 1.

- Choose an activity from the suggestions below, or plan your own activity by adapting one of them.

- Work your way through the vocabulary list one or two at a time. Back up the activities with very simple stories.

- You will need to reinforce the understanding of these words continually. Use the target word or words in general classroom instructions.

- Examples of useful books can be found in Resources, pp261–2.

TEACHING IDEAS

1 **TEACHING TARGET: to understand** *morning, after, afternoon*

▶ **Construction & craft**

Paper, pens, Special Calendar (Activity Sheet 7, Resources, pp243–5)

Help the child make some new moveable stick-on pictures for the Special Calendar of things which happen regularly during the week (assembly, music, story, Golden Time). Start every morning by visiting the calendar and choosing a stick-on picture of something that is going to happen during the day. It can be something that is going to happen in the *morning*, in the *afternoon*, or *after* dinner. Point out carefully to the child where the picture is to go ('Look, we will be having Golden Time this *morning.*' or 'See, we will have music this *afternoon*, *after* dinner.') Then stick the picture on the appropriate part of the day before or after the 'lunchtime' picture.

2 **TEACHING TARGET: to understand** *morning, after, afternoon*

▶ **Construction & craft**

Paper, pens, Special Calendar (Activity Sheet 7, Resources, pp243–5)

Identify something special and outside normal routine that is going to happen during the week. Let the child help you make the stick-on picture. When the day of the event comes, help him stick the picture on the Special Calendar in the right place. ('We will be going swimming this *morning*, *after* snack time', or 'We will be going swimming this *afternoon*, *after* lunch.' 'We will be going on the trip this *morning.*')

If possible, revisit the calendar after the event has taken place and point out: 'See, we went swimming *after* lunch, didn't we?'

3 **TEACHING TARGET: to understand** *birthday*

▶ **Construction & craft**

Card, colouring pencils, Special Calendar (Activity Sheet 7, Resources, pp243–5)

Help the child to make a stick-on birthday picture (cake and candles, balloons). When it is somebody's birthday, find the birthday picture and stick it on the Special Calendar. ('Today it is Harry's *birthday*. He is 5 – count my fingers, one, two, three, four, five.')

4 **TEACHING TARGET: to understand *birthday, tomorrow, today***

▶ **Construction & craft**

Paper, pens, Special Calendar (Activity Sheet 7, Resources, pp243–5)

The day before the child's own birthday, help him make an extra-special stick-on picture with the appropriate number of candles on the cake. Show him how to put it on the Special Calendar for the next day. Talk about it being his *birthday tomorrow* and how old he is going to be.

The next day you will be able to say, 'It's your *birthday today.* Look, here's your *birthday* picture.'

5 **TEACHING TARGET: to understand *holiday***

▶ **Construction & craft**

Pictures showing holiday activities, colours, holiday pictures to colour in

Explain that *holiday* means 'no school!' and talk about what the child might do on his *holiday.* Sometimes it means going away from home to somewhere special. Get him to colour in a *holiday* picture of his choice.

6 **TEACHING TARGET: to understand *holiday, tomorrow***

▶ **Construction & craft**

Paper, pens, Special Calendar (Activity Sheet 7, Resources, pp243–5)

Use an idea that the child seemed interested in and/or familiar with when you were talking about holidays. Help him make a stick-on holiday picture for the Special Calendar.

The day before the holiday begins, help him put the stick-on picture on the next day's space ('*Tomorrow* is a *holiday.* No school!').

7 **TEACHING TARGET: to understand *birthday, morning***

▶ **Storybooks**

A storybook about a child having a birthday

Read a simple story about a child's birthday.

8 **TEACHING TARGET: to understand *holiday***

▶ **Storybooks**

A storybook about a child or family going on holiday

Read a simple story about a child or a family going on holiday.

UNDERSTANDING TIME WORDS
STAGE THREE

ACTIVITY AREAS
▶ Construction & craft
▶ Storybooks

VOCABULARY

yesterday	before
days of the week	later/later on
weekend	next
not yet	

WHAT TO DO

Most of these activity suggestions involve using the Special Calendar (Activity Sheet 7, Resources, pp243–5). If you have not already made one of these, you will need to do so now.

- Choose one of the activities suggested below, or plan your own activity by adapting one of them.

- Work your way through the vocabulary list one or two at a time. You will need to reinforce these words continually, and use target words during general classroom instructions.

TEACHING IDEAS

1 **TEACHING TARGET: to understand** *yesterday*

▶ **Construction & craft**

Special Calendar (Activity Sheet 7, Resources, pp243–5), paper, pens

If you have not been working on Time Words previously with this child, look back at Stages One and Two. Visit the Special Calendar first thing every morning. Help the child make some more stick-on pictures of things that happen every week, and any special events that are planned. Continue to talk regularly about today and tomorrow as in Stage Two, but now introduce the idea of yesterday as well. On Tuesday, look back at Monday's pictures and say, 'This is what we did *yesterday'*, or 'This is what happened *yesterday.'* Then remove yesterday's pictures. Similarly, on Wednesday look back at Tuesday's pictures, and so on through the week.

2 **TEACHING TARGET: to understand** *before*

▶ **Construction & craft**

Special Calendar (Activity Sheet 7, Resources, pp243–5)

Visit the Special Calendar daily. Each time choose a stick-on picture that is going to happen that day (*today*). Tell the child, for example, 'We will have music *before* snack time' and help him stick the picture on in the right place. It is helpful to have a second picture of something that is going to happen *after* snack time to stick on as well, to provide a contrast.

3 **TEACHING TARGET: to understand days of the week,** *yesterday*

▶ **Construction & craft**

Special Calendar (Activity Sheet 7, Resources, pp243–5), card or paper, colours

Help the child write the name of a day of the week on each section of the Special Calendar. Alternatively, you might like to make the letters separately, get the child to colour them, and stick them on. Visit the calendar daily, and tell the child: 'Today is *Monday/Tuesday/Wednesday'* as appropriate. Show him the word as well as saying it. Combine this with teaching about yesterday ('*Yesterday* was *Monday.'*)

4 **TEACHING TARGET: to understand days of the week**

▶ **Storybooks**

A storybook about things happening on different days of the week

(*Note: Activity 3 must be done before this one.*)

Read the story and relate it to the Special Calendar (Activity Sheet 7, Resources, pp243–5). ('Look, Tom went to the park on *Monday*. What did we do on *Monday*? We went on our trip.')

5 **TEACHING TARGET: to understand *later (on), next***

▶ **Construction & craft**

Special Calendar (Activity Sheet 7, Resources, pp243–5)

Decide on a particular day of the week for this activity and think of two things for which you have pictures that are going to happen that day. When the first one is due, go to the calendar, find the appropriate picture, and tell the child: 'We are going to do this *next*.' Help him stick the picture on the right part of the calendar day. Then find a second picture of something due to occur later on and help the child to stick it in the right place ('We're going to do that *later*.')

6 **TEACHING TARGET: to understand *weekend***

▶ **Construction & craft**

Special Calendar (Activity Sheet 7, Resources, pp243–5)

Discuss with the child things he likes which happen at the weekend. Try to find out something special that is going to happen at the weekend. You may like to give the child a Home-School book, which enables parents and teachers to share interesting events in the child's life. Help the child make a stick-on picture to illustrate the special event. Stick it on either the Saturday or Sunday space, or if you are not sure when it is going to be, across the two. ('You're going to do this at the *weekend*, when you don't come to school.') Do this every week. On Monday, consult the Home-School book, visit the calendar, and say 'You did so-and-so at the *weekend*.'

UNDERSTANDING TIME WORDS
STAGE FOUR

ACTIVITY AREAS ▶

- ▶ Daily activities
- ▶ Games
- ▶ Construction & craft
- ▶ Storybooks
- ▶ Tabletop games

VOCABULARY

always	every day
never	often
usually	sometimes
early	late
long ago	evening
a long time	

WHAT TO DO

Many of these teaching ideas involve using a Special Calendar (Activity Sheet 7, Resources, pp243–5). If you have not already made one of these, you need to do so now, and to look back at how it was used in Stages Two and Three.

- Choose a target word or group of words.

- Choose one of the activities suggested below, or plan your own activity by adapting one of them.

- Work your way through the vocabulary list one or two at a time. You will need to reinforce all these words continually. Use the target words in general classroom instructions.

TEACHING IDEAS

1 **TEACHING TARGET: to understand always, every day**

▶ **Construction & craft**

Special Calendar (Activity Sheet 7, Resources, pp243–5)

Visit the Special Calendar. Encourage the child to point to each day. 'Can you find things that happen *every day*, that you *always* do? You *always* get up in the morning. You *always* go to bed at night. You *always* get dressed in the morning. You *always* have something to eat for dinner. Christmas Day is *always* on the same date in December.' Stick on missing items, or remove inappropriate ones.

2 **TEACHING TARGET: to understand never**

▶ **Games**

None

Help the child think of some dangerous things that we never, never, never do. 'We *never* put our hands down on a hot stove. We *never* run across the road without looking. We *never* play with very sharp things.' Then encourage the child or children to think of some ridiculous things that *never*, *never* happen. 'We *never* eat worms. We *never* go down rabbit holes. Giraffes *never* come to tea.' Keep a note of the suggestions. Can you get to ten ideas between you?

3 **TEACHING TARGET: to understand early, late**

▶ **Construction & craft**

Special Calendar (Activity Sheet 7, Resources, pp243–5), Blu-tack, fuzzy felt

Visit the Special Calendar. Give the child bits of Blu-tack or fuzzy felt without pictures. Show him how to stick a bit on the *early* part of each day and a bit on the *late* part – bedtime or after. Talk about who gets up *early* in the day (you might say before breakfast) – birds, postmen, milkmen? 'Who goes to bed really *late* – grownups?' Talk about being *too early* or *too late*. 'What would happen if you were *too early* for school?' It would be all locked up. There would be nobody there. 'And if you were *too late* to catch the bus or train?' It would have gone without you.

④ TEACHING TARGET: to understand *always, usually, often, sometimes*

▶ **Tabletop games**

Four separate cards, one marked: 'always' (marked with a red dot), one 'usually' (blue dot), one 'often' (green dot) and one 'sometimes' (yellow dot). Red, blue, green and yellow counters. A list of events to correspond with the target words (Examples: We always have a snack in the morning/go to bed at night/wear clothes. We usually go out to play at dinner time/have assembly in the morning. We often have apples for snack time/do PE/have Golden Time. We sometimes go swimming/out on trips.) On your events list make sure you have a good selection of the 'always' events, fewer of the 'usually' ones, fewer still of 'often', and fewest of the 'sometimes' events.

Read out the events one by one, and ask the children to put a counter on the appropriate card by matching counter to coloured dot (eg red counters on the 'always' card). Explain as you go that *always* means every day, *usually* means nearly every day, *often* means quite a lot of times, and *sometimes* means not very often.

When you have used up your list of events, show the children that there are lots of counters on the *always* card, not quite so many on the *usually* card, fewer still on the *often* card, and fewest on the *sometimes* one.

⑤ TEACHING TARGET: to understand *long ago*

▶ **Storybooks**

A storybook about 'olden times'

Many children of this age have a very hazy idea of long ago. Introduce the idea with a story or stories about things that no longer happen (dinosaurs, knights fighting on horseback, sea battles between sailing ships, people living in caves and wearing skins). Start off with 'Once upon a time, a long, long time ago.' When you move on to teaching weeks, months and years on the calendar, you can begin to give the children some slight idea of how far back 'long ago' might be. At this stage just indicate that these things don't happen any more.

⑥ TEACHING TARGET: to understand *evening*

▶ **Construction & craft**

Special Calendar (Activity Sheet 7, Resources, pp243–5), card, pens

If the child has a Home-school Book find out what his routine is in the early evening. If that is the time he watches television, for example, make two or three stick-on pictures of a television for the Special Calendar. Get the child to attach them to each day just before the 'bedtime' picture. Talk about what he does in the *evening* – that's just before it's night-time and he goes to bed.

UNDERSTANDING STORIES
STAGE ONE

 **ACTIVITY AREAS** ▶
- ▶ Pictures
- ▶ Songs & rhymes
- ▶ Picture books
- ▶ Storybooks

WHAT TO DO

Observe the child over a few days to see what his favourite play activities are. Make a list of these activities.

- Use the teaching ideas below. They are in developmental order. You may need to repeat each activity several times and also plan your own variations before moving on to the next one.

- Examples of useful books can be found in Resources, pp261–2.

TEACHING IDEAS

1 **TEACHING TARGET: to enjoy recognising toys in pictures**

▶ **Pictures**

 A collection of large pictures of everyday objects including two or three favourite toys

Seat the child beside you, turn the pictures over one by one, naming the objects until you come to a well-liked toy. Then say, for example: 'Oh look! Bricks! Let's go and find some.' The session then becomes a short play session with the bricks. Repeat this activity every day if possible, varying the type of toy, until the child begins to associate the pictures with the toys and starts to search for particular pictures. Then offer him the choice of toy to play with from three or four pictures. Spread the pictures out in front of him and encourage him by saying, 'Which one shall we have?' and pointing to the pictures in turn.

2 **TEACHING TARGET: to be able to match objects to pictures**

▶ **Pictures**

Five or six toys and matching pictures

Place the first picture on the floor or table and help the child to find the matching toy and put it on the picture. Encourage him to do this with all the toys. Help, cajole or structure him as much as necessary until the task is complete. Give lots of praise and whatever reward has been decided on – a short play session perhaps. Once he begins to enjoy the activity, include pictures and objects other than toys – for example, a cup, an apple, a chair, a brush and encourage him to place the objects on the pictures.

3 **TEACHING TARGET: to be able to associate a picture with a favourite song or rhyme**

▶ **Songs & rhymes**

Some simple pictures to represent familiar rhymes (eg a bus for 'The Wheels on the Bus', a spider for 'Incy Wincy Spider', a boat for 'Row, Row, Row your Boat'.)

Select one of the rhyme pictures that you have made and show it to the child. Say, for example: 'Look! A bus! Let's sing "The Wheels on the Bus".' Work your way on a daily basis through four or five songs. Once you think the child has begun to associate the pictures with the songs, let him choose which one you will sing by spreading out a few of the pictures and letting him choose which one he wants by pointing.

4 **TEACHING TARGET: to be able to attend briefly to a picture book**

▶ **Picture books**

A lift-the-flap or pop-up book with large clear pictures

Seat the child beside you, so he can help turn the pages but you can stop him turning over the next page until you are ready. Go through the book page by page, adding a little anticipation and excitement by holding down each page and saying, 'What's it going to be? What do you think? A ball? A dog? Let's see' and then turning over.

5 **TEACHING TARGET: to be able to recognise pictures of simple actions**

▶ **Pictures**

 Large pictures of simple actions (eg *Early Actions* cards from ColorCards®, Resources p263), a teddy or large doll

Turn over the pictures one at a time, and make the toy perform the action in the picture. Say what the toy is doing ('Look, he's jumping'). Make it as dramatic and as much fun as you can. Move on to doing the actions with the child.

6 **TEACHING TARGET: to be able to attend briefly to a very simple story**

▶ **Picture books**

 A simple story about a short series of real life events

Some examples of the real life events might be a child getting up in the morning, getting dressed, going downstairs, having breakfast; a child going to the park, playing on a swing, a seesaw, a slide, then having an ice cream and going home; a child going for a walk with dad, meeting a cat, feeding the ducks on the pond, seeing some children in a sandpit, seeing a fire engine, splashing in a puddle. Read the story slowly, page by page, letting the child have a good look at each picture, and keeping the language to a minimum.

UNDERSTANDING STORIES
STAGE TWO

ACTIVITY AREAS  ▶ Storybooks

WHAT TO DO

Arrange to withdraw the child from the class Story Time to start with.

- Check the child's level of receptive language and keep it in mind when choosing the stories. Explain any words you think he will not understand.

- Work through the teaching ideas in the order given, repeating each idea with several different books before moving on.

- Examples of useful books can be found in Resources, pp261–2.

TEACHING IDEAS

1 **TEACHING TARGET: to enjoy a short story one to one in a quiet area**

▶ **Storybooks**

 Lift-the-flap, peephole or pop-up type storybook with pictures.

Take the child to a quiet area and read him the story. Go slowly and let him have plenty of time to look at the pictures, lift the flap or move the lever as appropriate. Spend a minute or two talking about the story when you get to the end.

2 **TEACHING TARGET: to enjoy a familiar short story with one or two other children in a quiet area**

▶ **Storybooks**

 Lift-the-flap or similar book the child is familiar with

Take the child with one or two others to a quiet area. Read them the story, and let the child help show the pictures and tell as much about the story as he can.

3 **TEACHING TARGET: to attend to and enjoy a new short story with one or two other children in a quiet area**

▶ **Storybooks**

 A new lift-the-flap or simple book

Take the child with one or two others to a quiet area. Read them the story.

4 **TEACHING TARGET: to attend to and enjoy a familiar short story in a corner of the classroom**

▶ **Storybooks**

 A familiar lift-the-flap or simple book

Seat the child in the quietest available corner of the classroom, preferably away from passageways, doors to the toilets, windows. Read him the story as usual.

5 **TEACHING TARGET: to join the whole class and attend to a short story**

▶ **Storybooks**

 Find out when an easy story is going to be read to the group, and read it first with the child

During the whole class Story Time, seat the child where the reader can maintain good eye contact with him and from where he is able to see the pictures easily when they are shown round. If he is a child who finds sitting still very difficult, he may manage better if seated on a chair at the back of the circle, rather than on the carpet.

(6) TEACHING TARGET: to join the whole class and attend to the chosen story occasionally

▶ **Storybooks**

 None

By now the child should occasionally be able to attend to and enjoy the same story as the rest of the class. If the chosen story is clearly too much for his vocabulary and/or attention control, encourage him to sit through it, enjoy the pictures and get what he can from it, but arrange for one of 'his' special stories to be read as well. Go over the story he found difficult at a later time with him on his own.

Continue to give him opportunities to hear new stories suited to his ability level, on his own, or in a small group.

UNDERSTANDING STORIES
STAGE THREE

ACTIVITY AREAS    ▶ Storybooks

WHAT TO DO

Identify a range of suitable storybooks. These should have pictures every two or three pages and they should be about things that interest the child and in language he can understand. Alternatively, just show him the pictures a bit less often.

TEACHING IDEAS

1 **TEACHING TARGET: to be able to maintain attention and interest in a book with fewer pictures in a one-to-one situation**

▶ **Storybooks**

 Two or three selected books

Let the child choose one of the books. Read it with him in a one-to-one situation, explaining unknown words and stopping as often as necessary to maintain attention. Repeat this activity on several occasions with differing selections of books.

2 **TEACHING TARGET: to be able to maintain attention and interest in a book with fewer pictures in whole class Story Time**

▶ **Storybooks**

 None

Arrange to have one of the books you have gone through with the child read in whole class Story Time. Seat the child in the circle where the reader can maintain eye contact with him, and where he can see the pictures easily when they are shown round. If he is a child who finds maintaining attention very difficult, try seating him on a chair at the back of the circle.

3 **TEACHING TARGET: to be able to maintain attention and interest in unfamiliar books with relatively few pictures**

▶ **Storybooks such as *The Tiger Who Came To Tea* (Resources, p262)**

 None

At this stage the child should be able to follow and enjoy a story without pre-teaching. If he finds a particular story difficult and loses interest, go over it with him afterwards, explaining unfamiliar words and talking it through.

UNDERSTANDING STORIES
STAGE FOUR

ACTIVITY AREAS  ▶ Storybooks

WHAT TO DO

There are no specific activities for this stage. The child may still find following the stories difficult because of one or more of the following:

- His attention control is not adequate for the sustained listening required.

- He doesn't understand many of the words.

- He loses the main thread of the story because he gets bogged down trying to understand words or sentences.

- He cannot make inferences.

Ways to help

1 Read the story substituting simpler language where necessary.

2 Explain the meaning of words the child obviously doesn't understand.

3 Shorten long sentences.

4 Explain when something is implied but not spelt out. For example, the story says: 'The bone lay on the stairs where Jock had left it.' We infer that Jock is a dog. Or the story may say: 'Mum called out that Jamie was going to be late again.' We assume that Jamie has been late before.

5 If after trying numbers 1–4 the child is still confused, tell the whole story in your own words.

- Pre-teach stories as indicated *before* they are read to the whole class. This gives confidence and improves the child's listening and attention.

- Once the child's understanding and listening skills have begun to improve, change to re-reading the stories *after* they have been read to the whole class. It may then be possible to spot exactly where and why the child has had difficulty understanding.

> *If the child consistently has difficulty in drawing inferences (and has difficulty understanding the meaning of idioms and metaphors such as 'pull your socks up' and 'good as gold'), it is possible that he has either a language disorder or an autistic spectrum disorder. In either case he should be assessed by an educational psychologist and a speech & language therapist.*

PART II ACTIVITIES FOR USING LANGUAGE

CHECKLIST FOR PART II: USING LANGUAGE

	P Scale 5/6 Stage One 2–3 years equivalent	P Scale 6/7 Stage Two 3–4 years equivalent	P Scale 7/8 Stage Three 4–4.5 years equivalent	NC Level 1+ Stage Four 4.5–5 years equivalent
NAMING WORDS	Only uses words relating to himself	Only uses vocabulary relating to everyday things	Use of vocabulary still restricted	Use of vocabulary restricted and does not use category names
ACTION WORDS	Only uses action words relating to himself	Only uses action words for everyday activities	Use of action vocabulary still restricted	
ASKING QUESTIONS	Only asks questions by intonation (It teatime?) or occasional What? questions	Does not use Where? or Which? questions	Cannot ask Who?, Why? or When? questions	Does not ask How? questions
GRAMMAR	Grammar is not important at this developmental stage	Does not use /s/ to mark plurals (cat/cats)	Does not use past tense marker – ed (jump/ jumped)	Does not use irregular past tenses or irregular plurals (ran, flew, children, men)
TALKING IN SENTENCES	Uses mainly single- or two-word sentences	Does not use three-word sentences	Sentences not longer than four-five words / Does not use and to link sentences	Does not use or, if, when, so, but, because in sentences

USING NAMING WORDS
STAGE ONE

ACTIVITY AREAS
- ► Home Corner
- ► Songs & rhymes
- ► Games
- ► Picture books
- ► Small toy play

VOCABULARY

Myself	eyes, nose, mouth, feet, hands, hair, fingers
Clothes	child's everyday clothes
People	man, lady (woman), boy, girl, baby
Household	bed, chair, table, cup, spoon, plate
Food	apple, orange, juice, milk, biscuit, bread, sandwich
Vehicles	car, bus, bike, taxi, lorry, plane
Animals	cat, dog, horse, cow, pig, rabbit, sheep
Inside	kitchen, bathroom, bedroom, living room, toilet, classroom, hall
Outside	field, gate, house, wall, playground
Toys	brick, ball, sand, water, teddy, doll
School items	pencils, paper, paints, glue, scissors

WHAT TO DO

The vocabulary list in the box is just a start. You can add other early naming words as they crop up.

- Choose words from one or more of the vocabulary groups, not more than five or six words at a time.

- Check that the child understands the words. Name the objects or people in a picture, and see if the child can point to them.

- Choose one of the activities suggested below, or plan your own activity by adapting one of them.

- Work your way through the vocabulary list a few at a time. You may have to teach some of the words in several different ways on several different occasions.

TEACHING IDEAS

1 **TEACHING TARGET: to use the words** *teddy, doll, bed, chair, cup, spoon*

▶ **Home Corner**

 Large teddies, dolls

Extended play with the big toys. Model the words you want the child to try to use. 'Come here *Teddy*. Sit on your *chair*. Here's your *cup*. Here's your *spoon*.' 'Show your teddy his *spoon*. Give him his *cup*.' 'Tell him where to sit.'

2 **TEACHING TARGET: to use the names of animals**

▶ **Songs & rhymes**

 Toy farm animals

Sing 'Old MacDonald had a Farm' (Resources, p225). Repeat it on several days until it becomes really familiar. Each time you name an animal in the song, hold up the appropriate toy. 'Old MacDonald had a farm, and on that farm he had a *cow*' (holding up the cow at the same time). Once you think the child knows the song, use the cloze procedure (Resources, p228). Sing the song, and when you get to an animal name stop singing and just hold up the appropriate toy, looking expectantly at the child to supply the missing word. If you have a group of children, you might give each child a toy animal, and let them take turns to fill in the missing animal names. (You can use lots of action rhymes or songs in this way, provided you can find some way to illustrate the key words. For example, 'Humpty Dumpty' – key word 'wall'; build a little wall with bricks and have a toy Humpty. 'Baa Baa Black Sheep – key word 'sheep'; have a toy sheep. 'Incy Wincy Spider' – key word 'spider'; have a toy spider.) It doesn't matter if the child can't really join in the rest of the song or rhyme, but remember to go slowly enough for him to attempt the key words.

3 **TEACHING TARGET: to use the words** *cup, spoon, brick, ball, book, car*

▶ **Games – Feely bag game (Resources, p218)**

A feely bag and objects to match, which need to have distinctive shapes

This game is more fun for a small group than for one child. Show the objects to the children first and name them. Then put one object in the bag. Ask the first child to come and have a feel. Can he guess what it is? Can he tell you its name? Repeat with another object and another child. If they are stuck, prompt them by doing little mimes and saying, 'You drink from a …' or 'You read a …' Give several turns each.

④ TEACHING TARGET: to use the words *car, bus, taxi, lorry, plane, bike*

▶ **Games**

Toy vehicles

Show the vehicles to the children and name them. Then hide them around the room and send the children off to find them. When they come back with a 'find', ask them what they found. If they need prompting, say 'It's a *car*. You found a …' or 'It's a *plane*. You found a …'

⑤ TEACHING TARGET: to use a selection of words from the list, or your own additions

▶ **Picture books**

A book with pictures showing lots of objects and actions

Find, for example, a picture of a park. Find a dog in the picture and point to it, saying 'Here's a *dog*. Any more *dogs* anywhere? Can you find a *dog*?' Encourage the child to find as many as he can and use the word. Then find something else, perhaps a bird, a boat or a duck. Each time encourage the child to find some more and name them following your model.

⑥ TEACHING TARGET: to use the words *apple, orange, banana, biscuit, juice, milk*

▶ **Home corner**

Toy food, a large soft toy for each child, a glove puppet

Seat the children round the table with their toys beside them. Use the forced alternative technique (Resources, p228). Make your puppet say to the first child, 'Does your teddy want an *apple* or an *orange*?' as you hold out both fruits. Give the child the item he asks for. Say to the next child, 'Does monkey want a *biscuit* or a *banana*?' holding out the two choices again, one in each hand. Continue until all the food has been distributed. Then have a toy tea party.

USING NAMING WORDS
STAGE TWO

ACTIVITY AREAS ▶

- ▶ Songs & rhymes
- ▶ Dressing up
- ▶ Games

- ▶ Small toy play
- ▶ Picture books
- ▶ Tabletop games

VOCABULARY

Myself	lips, tongue, head, teeth, chin, knee, shoulder, toes, arms, legs, knees
Clothes	boots, hat, anorak, vest, sandals, gloves, scarf
People	postman, policeman, doctor, nurse, dentist, teacher
Household	phone, cooker, kettle, clock, fridge, sink, TV, settee, cupboard
Food	eggs, beans, cake, carrot, banana, jam
Vehicles	helicopter, tractor, motorbike, plane, train, lorry
Animals	fish, hamster, bird, elephant, giraffe, camel
Inside	walls, stairs, curtains, carpets, doors, pictures
Outside	trees, roads, shops, garage, station, park, farm, gate
Toys	Lego, skipping rope, roller skates, kite, swing, slide
School items	ruler, rubber, reading book, storybook
Weather	rain, wind, sun, ice, snow, frost, thunder

WHAT TO DO

Choose words from one or more of the vocabulary groups, four or five at a time. You can add more words as they crop up.

- Check that the child understands the words? (Can he point to them in a picture if you name them for him?)

- Choose one of the activities suggested below, or plan your own activity by adapting one of them.

- Work your way through the vocabulary list a few at a time. You may have to teach some of the words in several different ways on several different occasions.

TEACHING IDEAS

1 **TEACHING TARGET: to use the words** *rain(drops), thunder*

▶ **Songs & rhymes**

An umbrella, a drum

Sing the song 'I Hear Thunder' (Resources, p225). Do a roll on the drum for the thunder and use your fingers to imitate the raindrops coming down. When the children know the song really well, use the cloze procedure (Resources, p228) for them to fill in the words 'thunder' and 'raindrops' ('I hear ...'). 'Raindrops' is a hard word to say, and you might want to substitute 'raining'. Accept any rough attempt at the words.

2 **TEACHING TARGET: to use the words** *postman, doctor, nurse,* **etc.**

▶ **Dressing up/Storybooks**

A dressing-up outfit for each child

Offer the children the forced alternative choice (Resources, p228) 'Do you want to be a postman or a doctor?' 'Do you want to be a doctor or a nurse?' When they are all dressed up, encourage some acting out of their respective roles. Follow up with a story about one or other character, perhaps Postman Pat, using the cloze procedure (Resources, p228) for the children to fill in 'postman' ('He's a ...')

3 **TEACHING TARGET: to use the words for a selection of small objects**

▶ **Games**

Ten small objects, a 'shopping' bag

Play the Shopping Game (Resources, p219). Send the children off in turn to fetch one item from the 'shop' for you (say eg 'Fetch me a crayon.') When the child returns with it in his bag, ask him 'What have you got?' Model the word for him again if he is stuck. ('You got a *crayon* – what is it?') Replace the crayon in the 'shop' before the next child has a turn.

④ TEACHING TARGET: to use the words *train, lorry, tractor, plane, helicopter, motorbike*

▶ **Small toy play**

Vehicles, playmat

Tell the child you are going to share out the toys before you start playing. Hold out two vehicles, one in each hand, and say 'Do you want the train or the lorry?' (forced alternative). Repeat with the rest of the vehicles until you have half the toys each. Then have an extended play session.

⑤ TEACHING TARGET: to use the words *park, garage, road, shop, station*

▶ **Picture books**

A book with large pictures showing a town or city scene

Talk about it with the child. Then ask him to find you something in the picture. Say, eg, 'Can you find a shop?' When the child points to one, say 'What is it? It's a …'. Model it for him again if he can't fill in the word. ('It's a *shop* – what is it?) Stop after four or five words unless the child is keen to continue.

⑥ TEACHING TARGET: to use the words for a collection of items

▶ **Tabletop games**

A set of paired cards showing pictures of target words

First sort the cards into pairs and make them into a deck so that you will turn up two identical pictures, then two more identical pictures, and so on. Take turns to turn up a card. You go first, saying, for example, 'It's a dog.' Encourage the child to turn up the next picture and tell you what it is. Point out to him that they are the same. Now introduce the Pairs Game (Resources, p219). Play in the usual way, but be sure that everyone names each picture as they turn it over.

USING NAMING WORDS
STAGE THREE

ACTIVITY AREAS ▶
- ▶ Games
- ▶ Tabletop games
- ▶ Paper & pencil

VOCABULARY AND CATEGORY NAMES

Body	ankle, elbow, chest, wrist, neck, eyebrows, eyelashes
Jobs, professions	builder, plumber, teacher, doctor, shopkeeper, engineer, soldier, sailor, carpenter
Furniture	cupboard, wardrobe, chest, stool, bunk bed, armchair
Vehicles, transport	van, moped, boat, liner, yacht, hovercraft
Creatures	goat, duck, goose, hippo, seal, beetle, goldfish
Sports and games	football, rugby, tennis, swimming, chess, skating, motor racing, horse racing, skiing
Buildings	houses, flats, offices, castles, barns, stables
Food	lemons, grapefruit, cabbage, lettuce, meat, butter, pies, sausages, bacon, pastry, buns
Seasons	spring, summer, autumn, winter

WHAT TO DO

Choose words from any category or several different ones. You can add more words as they crop up. Stress the category names themselves (Body, Jobs, Vehicles).

- Check that the children understand the words by asking them to point to pictures when you name them. Talk about words that are unfamiliar to them.

- Choose one of the activities suggested below, or plan your own activity by adapting one of them.

- Work your way through the vocabulary list a few at a time. You may have to teach some of the words in several different ways and on several different occasions.

TEACHING IDEAS

1 **TEACHING TARGET: to use the words for various jobs, professions**

▶ **Games**

Cards with descriptions of jobs and professions, pictures of builders, dentists, doctors, teachers, etc (see Activity Sheet 17, Resources, p259)

Write out brief descriptions of what the various jobs and professions entail on cards, and give one to each child. Help each child in turn to read out the descriptions. Hands up who knows what job or profession you are describing. Can anyone tell you anything more about it? Prompt where necessary ('It's a doc…'). Use pictures as necessary to help understanding.

2 **TEACHING TARGET: to use the words for various foods**

▶ **Games**

Pictures of different foods or toy food, a bag

Put the pictures or objects in a box or bag. Challenge the children to name ten different kinds of food as you hold up the pictures or objects. Hold up the first one for a child to identify. If he is stuck, clap out the name (cab-bage: two claps, cau-lif-flow-er: four claps, let-tuce: two claps). If he is still stuck, give him the initial letter sound ('It's a l…, it's a c…' and clap the syllables as well. If you have enough children playing, you can make this into a competitive team game.

3 **TEACHING TARGET: to use the words for furniture items**

▶ **Games**

Ten items of doll's house furniture, a cloth to cover them

Play Kim's Game (Resources, p222). Put the objects on the table and cover them with a tea towel or cloth. Explain the game to the children. Then lift the cloth. Let them look at the objects for about 20 seconds. Cover them up again. Secretly remove one thing. Lift the cloth – who can tell you what is missing? Repeat, removing another item, and so on.

4 **TEACHING TARGET: to use the words for creatures**

▶ **Games – Barrier game (Resources, p218)**

Pictures of different creatures, a screen

Show the child how the game is played. Then give him a two- or three-picture set to match. See if he can remember even up to four. Then let him take the role of teacher. He sets out his pictures and tells you what pictures you have to choose to match his set. Mistakes on the part of the adult give great pleasure!

5 **TEACHING TARGET: to use words the children have found hard to say or hard to remember**

▶ **Games**

Pencil, paper, sticky labels, four small containers

Look through previous teaching sessions and consult the vocabulary lists. Help the children identify words they found hard to say. Write each word on a separate slip of paper in large, bold joined up writing or script, whichever the children are happiest with. Label the pots 1, 2, 3 and 4. Explain to the children that you are going to sort the words according to the number of syllables. If they are not yet familiar with the concept of syllables, clap out a few words to give them the idea. Then let somebody pick a slip to choose the first word. Say it and clap it at the same time (eg en-gin-eer, shop-kee-per, foot-ball). Ask the children to tell you how many syllables in that word.

Repeat the saying/clapping until they get the right number and put the slip into the appropriately marked pot. Repeat with the next word. Do this until you think the children are beginning to get the hang of it. Then drop the clapping and just say the words, slowly and deliberately. Can they still identify how many syllables there are and put the slips in the right pots? Finish up by helping the children to say and clap the words.

6 **TEACHING TARGET: to use the names of sports and games**

▶ **Paper & pencil – Word Web (Activity Sheet 16, Resources, pp257–8)**

Paper and coloured pencils

Help the children to make a word web or word wheel. You can use the Football Word Web as an example or photocopy the blank template to create your own. Choose a sport or game to put in the middle of the web. Then gradually build up the web with suggestions from the children. 'Which season is this sport played in? What might the weather be like? What do we wear to play it? What equipment do we need? What sort of building might it take place in? If we go to a match, how might we get there? What team do we support?' Write in the suggestions with a different colour for each child. You might like to go over it again when it's finished and see who had the most ideas.

USING NAMING WORDS
STAGE FOUR

ACTIVITY AREAS ▶

▶ Games
▶ Tabletop games
▶ Reference books

VOCABULARY

creatures	food
drinks	furniture
tools	jobs, professions
clothes	body parts
sports and games	vehicles

WHAT TO DO

The aim here is to teach the words that denote a whole group (eg tools) as well as the various items within that group (eg hammer, screwdriver, saw).

- Choose a category or a mix of category words.

- If you introduce unfamiliar words, be sure to explain their meaning.

- You can extend this stage by including additional categories and the words that belong to them if they occur in the curriculum (eg mammals, reptiles, dairy products, meat, vegetables).

- Ask the children frequently to try to name the category you are working on.

- Choose one of the activities suggested below, or plan your own activity by adapting one of them.

TEACHING IDEAS

1 **TEACHING TARGET: to use the words** *food, drink, furniture*

▶ **Games**

Pictures of food, drink, furniture

Quickfire Questions. Explain the game to the children. You are going choose a child, then hold up one of the pictures and ask, 'Is it food, drink or furniture?' The child answers, you select another card and another child, and repeat until everyone has had a turn. Go round again trying to speed things up. If the children manage well, try another round without giving them the category names, just asking 'What group (category, family) does it belong to?' Can they give the answer? Use only familiar categories for this game.

2 **TEACHING TARGET: to use the word** *creatures*

▶ **Games**

A list of creatures' names for reference

Tell the children this is a guessing game. Start them off by saying you are thinking of a *creature*. Then give clues, one at a time, until somebody puts their hand up to say they've guessed it. If they are right, you can give them a point. If they are wrong, point out why and continue to give clues until somebody gets it right. Repeat with another creature, and so on. (Example: Rabbit. It's small and brown. It has four legs. It can run fast. It can jump. It has long ears. It lives in a hole in the ground. It likes to eat lettuce. You can keep some kinds of these as pets.) Prompt the children: 'These were all … (creatures).'

3 **TEACHING TARGET: to use the words** *clothes, food, tools*

▶ **Games**

None

This game needs three or more children. Seat the children in a circle which includes you. Explain that you are all going to make a 'word chain'. Start it off by saying the name of an item of clothing. The next person must think of another one, and you keep going round the circle until somebody gets stuck. Then start another chain with food items. You might make this into a competition by giving the children five points each and deducting one every time they are the one to break the chain. Help as much as necessary. When each list dries up, ask the children 'Those were all … (clothes)' etc.

4 **TEACHING TARGET: to use the words *sports, jobs, professions***

▶ **Tabletop games**

Race Board (Activity Sheet 1, Resources, p233), enlarged and stuck on cardboard, die, counters, tokens, pictures of sports and jobs or professions, eg ColorCards® *Occupations*

This game needs at least two children. You need to photocopy the Race Board, enlarge it and stick it on card. Place the pack of pictures face down on the table. The children play the game, throwing the die in turn and moving their counter or token round the board. When they land on a star, they turn up a card from the pack and name it (eg. doctor/profession). If they fail to name it, they move back two squares. If they get it *nearly* right they move back one square. Landing on a happy or sad face means moving forward or backward one space. The winner is the one who reaches the end of the track first.

5 **TEACHING TARGET: to use the words *clothes, body parts, sports and games***

▶ **Tabletop games**

Snakes and Ladders board, die, counters, tokens, list of category items for reference

The children play the game, throwing the die in turn and moving their token round the board. When they have to go down a snake, you call out an item from your list and they must supply the name of that category. The winner is the first one 'home'. Example: You call out 'football' and the child should say 'sport'.

6 **TEACHING TARGET: to use the word *vehicles***

▶ **Reference books**

A book with good clear pictures of a variety of vehicles

First see how many of the vehicles in the picture the children can name. Then let them show you which ones they don't know the name of. Choose one, tell the children its name and explain what it is used for. Count to five. Who can remember the name and say it? If it's a hard one to remember or say, help the children clap-and-say it in unison with you. Then move on to another of the vehicles the children wanted to know about. Get the children to use the word 'vehicles' often.

USING ACTION WORDS
STAGE ONE

ACTIVITY AREAS ▶

- ▶ Home Corner
- ▶ Songs & rhymes
- ▶ Hall/PE
- ▶ Construction & craft

VOCABULARY

come (here)	go	move	run	stand (still/up)
walk	sit (down)	lie (down)	jump	fetch/get
bring	pick (up)	put (down)	hold	carry
lift (up)	eat	drink	wash	dry
brush	blow	sleep	wake up	pull
push	put (on)	take (off)	catch	throw
give	build	knock (down)	fall (down)	cry
laugh	cuddle	smile	kiss	like
want	stop	wait	watch	listen
look (at)	touch	play	find	wave
clap	show			

WHAT TO DO

The vocabulary list in the box is just a start. You can add other early action words as they crop up.

- Choose a small group of words with a common theme or that fit well into the same teaching activity. It is a good idea to use opposites when you can (eg pull/push, put on/take off, catch/throw).

- Check that the child understands the words. Can he do the actions when told, or point to the right action picture when you name it? In some cases you can only tell if he understands the word by observation.

- Choose one of the activities suggested below, or plan your own activity by adapting one of them.

- Work your way through the vocabulary list a few at a time. You may have to teach some of the words in several different ways on several different occasions.

TEACHING IDEAS

1 TEACHING TARGET: to use the words *sit down, lie down, sleep, wake up, lift up*

▶ **Home Corner**

Big dolls and teddies, chairs, beds, blankets

Extended play. Let the child lead the play, but ask from time to time what he would like you to do with the doll or teddy that you are playing with (eg 'What shall my teddy do? *Sit down*? *Lie down*?' Model the alternatives. Ask him 'Shall my dolly *wake up*? I can't wake her up. You tell her. Say "*Wake up* dolly".'

2 TEACHING TARGET: to use the words *fall down, jump up*

▶ **Songs & rhymes**

None

Sing 'Ring a Ring o' Roses' (Resources, p226). Go slowly and put lots of emphasis on the 'fall down' and 'jump up' bits. Don't expect the child to join in all the rest of the rhyme, but encourage him to shout out the target words.

3 TEACHING TARGET: to use the words *come back (fly away)*

▶ **Songs & rhymes**

None

Teach the children the rhyme 'Two Little Dicky Birds': 'Two little dicky birds, sitting on the wall, one named Peter, one named Paul. Fly away Peter, fly away Paul. Come back Peter, Come back Paul.' Do the 'magic' of making the 'birds' disappear and reappear (Resources, p223). Peter and Paul will only *come back* when the children call out to them.

④ TEACHING TARGET: to use the words *walk, stop, stand (still), sit down, lie down, jump*

▶ **Hall/PE**

A glove puppet

This game needs three or four children. First spread the children around the room and use the glove puppet to tell them what to do. '*Walk* – that's right. Now … *stop*! *Stand still*! *Sit down*.' Ask one of the children to make the puppet give the instructions. If he can manage this without help, well and good, but if he can't, whisper each instruction to him so that he can pass it on to the puppet.

⑤ TEACHING TARGET: to use the words *catch, throw, give*

▶ **Hall/PE**

A soft ball or beanbag

A game for a small group, four or five or more. Arrange the children in a circle and you stand in the middle. Say someone's name, say '*Catch*' and throw them the ball. Then say either '*Throw* it to …' or '*Give* it to …' Repeat this with several children. Then put a child in the middle to be the 'teacher' and help them to do as you have been doing. Accept just 'throw' or 'give' if the child can't say the whole sentence. Let everyone have a turn.

⑥ TEACHING TARGET: to use the words *put (on), take (off), build, knock (down)*

▶ **Construction & craft**

Bricks, Lego or Duplo

Extended play. Join the child in building towers. When your tower is getting really tall and looks likely to fall, hold out a brick and say 'Shall I put it on?' (Don't just accept a 'yes'. The magic words to make you do it are '*Put it on*!') Hold the tower steady and put on a brick each time the child tells you. When the tower can't survive any longer, ask 'Shall we knock it down?' Again, only accept '*Knock*' or '*Knock down*' as the signal to do so. Then ask 'Shall we build it again?' and encourage the child to say '*build*'.

USING ACTION WORDS
STAGE TWO

ACTIVITY AREAS
- ▶ Songs & rhymes
- ▶ Hall/PE
- ▶ Games
- ▶ Construction & craft
- ▶ Tabletop games
- ▶ Storybooks

VOCABULARY

climb	ride	drive	kick
skip	hop	tip	fill
pour	cut	fit	write
draw	read	stick	glue
colour	paint	copy	talk
tell	whisper	shout	scream
ask	share	point	show
take	pass	take (turns)	make
turn (round)	help	feel	pat
squash	squeeze	roll	bang
shake	tap	dance	swim
race	kneel	start	move
leave (alone)	crawl	put (in)	

WHAT TO DO

Choose a small group of words with a common theme, or that will fit well together in a teaching activity. You can add more words to the list in the box.

- Check that the children understand the words. Can they carry out the action when told, or point to the right action in a picture?

- Choose one of the activities suggested below, or plan your own activity by adapting one of them.

- Work your way through the vocabulary list a few at a time. You may have to teach some of the words in several different ways on several different occasions.

TEACHING IDEAS

① **TEACHING TARGET: to use the words** *put, shake, turn (around)*

▶ **Songs & rhymes**

 None

Sing and act the 'Hokey Cokey' (Resources, p224). When the children have done it a few times, go really slowly on the key words and encourage them to start joining in.

② **TEACHING TARGET: to use the words** *hop, skip, jump, crawl, climb*

▶ **Hall/PE**

 Rope, PE apparatus

This really needs three or more children. Take the children through an obstacle course in which they have to crawl under a rope, jump over a rope, climb up two or three of the wall bars, skip two or three paces, and hop two or three steps. Then ask the children what they had to do. Give as much help as necessary.

③ **TEACHING TARGET: to use the words** *swim, pat, point, read, write, pour*

▶ **Games**

None

These strangely assorted words are chosen because they are not too difficult to mime. It will make a better game if you include some of the Stage One words as well (eg clap, eat, drink, wash, dry). Explain to the children that you are going to do a little acting and they have to guess what you are doing. Do your first action, choose a child to guess, and so on until everyone has had one or two turns. A confident child might like to take over as the actor and mime some actions for the others to guess. You can accept 'swim' or 'swimming'. If the child just says 'swim', you can model for him: 'That's right, I was swimming.'

4 **TEACHING TARGET: to use the words *squash, squeeze, pat, roll, bang***

▶ **Construction & craft**

Playdough or modelling clay

Help the children to make something of their own choosing. It might be a pancake, a bun, a little basket, a doughnut. Then get yourself a lump of playdough, and ask each child to tell you how to make something like theirs. Give them suggestions or forced alternatives. ('Do I *roll* it?' 'Do I *bang* it or *squash* it?' '*Pat* it?')

5 **TEACHING TARGET: to use the words *kneel, swim, dance, wave, clap, point, read, write***

▶ **Tabletop games**

Two sets of action picture cards or *Early Actions* ColorCards® (Resources, p263)

Play Snap in the normal way (Resources, p220) with a pack for each player. When a player has shouted 'snap', and before he claims his cards, he must name the action in the picture. Accept 'wave' rather than 'waving', or 'clap' rather than 'clapping', but confirm that the child is correct by saying, 'That's right, the boy's *waving*' or 'Yes, she's *clapping* her hands.'

6 **TEACHING TARGET: to use the words *can, run, catch***

▶ **Storybooks**

A suitable storybook

Read a simple story which includes a lot of repetition, for example *The Gingerbread Man* (Resources, p262). When the children have heard it once or twice, use the cloze procedure (Resources, p228). When you come to one of the repetitive bits (eg 'Run, run, as fast as you can') pause before the word 'can' and wait for the children to fill it in. ('Run, run as fast as you …You can't catch me, I'm the Gingerbread Man.') You can use this technique to prompt single words or whole phrases.

USING ACTION WORDS
STAGE THREE

ACTIVITY AREAS

▶ Songs & rhymes
▶ Games
▶ Picture books

▶ Storybooks
▶ Tabletop games

WHAT TO DO

Activities at this stage do not target specific words, but are intended to widen the verb vocabulary and develop increasing confidence in the use of verbs.

- Choose one of the activities suggested below, or plan your own activities by adapting some of them

TEACHING IDEAS

1 **TEACHING TARGET: to use a variety of action words in small phrases**

▶ **Songs & rhymes**

 None

Sing and act out 'If You're Happy and You Know It' (Resources, p224), introducing as many action words as practicable. Everybody joins in (eg 'If you're happy and you know it, *stamp your feet, touch your nose, wiggle your fingers, clap your hands, close your eyes, open your mouth, give a smile, wave your hand, fold your arms, point your finger*').

② TEACHING TARGET: to use a variety of action words in small phrases

▶ **Games**

None

Play 'Simon Says' (Resources, p223 and Activity Sheet 3, p237). By now the children should be able to play it the 'proper' way. Include as many actions as you can easily mime ('Simon says stand up/turn round/shake your hands'). After a turn or so with an adult taking the lead, let a child be 'Simon' and tell the others what Simon says.

③ TEACHING TARGET: to use action words starting with the same sound

▶ **Games**

List of sounds and action words

A game for three or more children. Seat them in a circle. The idea is for you to think of an initial letter sound and for the children in turn to think up an action word starting with that sound. Give them a sound and start them off (eg d – dance, drink, dry, dig, dash, draw, drive; w – wait, watch, whisper, wonder, whistle, wave, work). This is really quite difficult, so you will need to have your lists of sounds plus action words jotted down. When anybody is stuck give them a little mime as a clue. Try to get one action word out of everybody playing and more if possible.

④ TEACHING TARGET: to use some unfamiliar action words

▶ **Picture books**

A book showing lots of different activities

The children take turns to say what the people in the pictures are doing. When somebody finds an action that they don't recognise, or for which they do not know the word, see if anybody else can supply it. If not, introduce the word, explain its meaning and encourage talk about it. See if everyone can say the word. If it is a long word with several syllables, help the children say and clap it (eg ca-ra-van-ning, bi-cy-cling, hang-gli-ding, par-a-chu-ting).

⑤ TEACHING TARGET: to use action words in retelling a story

▶ **Storybooks**

An interesting and exciting storybook

Choose any interesting story that is within the children's range of understanding. Read it to the children with as much drama as you can muster. When you come to the end, ask the children in turn to tell you a little bit of what happened (eg 'What were the children doing? What happened next? What did the bear do? What did Daddy do?') until the story has been re-told. Encourage the children to use more than one-word answers.

⑥ TEACHING TARGET: to use action words

▶ **Table top games**

Race Board (Activity Sheet 1, Resources, p233) enlarged and copied onto card, action pictures, die, counters

Place the stack of action pictures face down on the table. Play the game in the usual way (Resources, p219), but when each child has made his move he must pick up a picture and say what the action is.

ASKING QUESTIONS
STAGE ONE

ACTIVITY AREAS ▶

▶ Games
▶ Home Corner
▶ Small toy play

QUESTION TYPES

What is it? What's that/this?

What's (in the box)?

What do you/does he want?

What has/have ... got?

What is/are ... doing?

WHAT TO DO

If the child is only using the occasional *what?* question, you will need to work through all these activities. Work through them in the order given, but reinforce each one either by playing the game two or three times, or by planning additional activities using ideas from the examples.

- In all these activities it is a great help to include one or two children with good language so that the child hears the modelled sentence lots of times.

TEACHING IDEAS

1 **TEACHING TARGET: to use the questions *What's this?*, *What's that?***

▶ **Games**

Two bags or boxes, some familiar and some less familiar objects

Into one bag you put a random collection of very familiar objects (cup, spoon, sock, doll, teddy bear etc.) Into the other put a collection of objects that are likely to be less familiar to the child, or unfamiliar (less usual fruits and vegetables from the toy food collection, a necklace, bracelet, scarf, toy helicopter/road roller/ digger). It doesn't matter if you happen to include a few items that the child does know the name of. You hold the bag of familiar objects while the child has the other one. Take turns to pull something out of the bag and ask each other '*What's this?*' (You can alternate this with '*What is it?*'). You go first to model the question. The child is expected to name the object. Then encourage him to take something out of his bag and ask you '*What's this?*' Prompt as much as necessary. (You can adapt this game to practise '*What's that?*' as well. Put two collections separately a little way away from you and the child and use a ruler to point at the objects.)

2 **TEACHING TARGET: to use the question *What's in the box?***

▶ **Games**

A collection of small, curious and interesting things (eg a marble, pretty stone, shell, brooch, tiny toy, box and a bag)

If you are working with one child on his own, put one of the little things in the box and one in the bag, without the child seeing them. Hold out the box and ask '*What's in the box?* Can you guess?' Let him have a guess or two and then do the same with the bag. Now prompt the child to ask '*What's in the bag?*' or '*What's in the box?*', whichever he likes first, and then the other one. Open the containers with a little flourish and show the contents. Repeat with the other objects. If you have two or three children in a group, let everybody have a turn at putting one object in the box and one in the bag, and everybody have a turn at asking '*What's in the bag?*' or '*What's in the box?*' Accept any attempt at the question as long as it includes the word *what* but keep modelling the correct question.

3 **TEACHING TARGET: to use the question *What have I got?***

▶ **Games**

A soft bag and a collection of objects of distinctive shape

Feely Bag game (Resources, p218). This game needs three or more children. Put one of the objects secretly in the bag and give it to the first child. He must offer the bag to one of the other children to have a feel. Prompt him to ask *'What have I got?'* Work your way through all the different objects. Let everybody have a turn at holding the bag and being the one to ask 'What have I got?' and let everybody have a turn at guessing. Model the question 'What have I got?' as often as necessary.

4 **TEACHING TARGET: to use the question *What is he doing?***

▶ **Games**

Doll or toy animal with movable limbs, a screen or barrier

You sit on one side of the screen with the toy, and the child sits on the other side. Make the toy perform some action. Prompt the child to ask *'What is he doing?'* When he makes a good try at asking the question (eg 'What doing?') lift the screen and make the toy repeat his action, the funnier the better. Explain to the child what the toy is doing. Repeat with as many actions as you can think of.

5 **TEACHING TARGET: to use the question *What are you doing?***

▶ **Small toy play**

Toy farm or zoo animals, farm or zoo, vehicles or garage

Get out a selection of small toys and share them out between you and the child. Once the child has started playing, turn your back on him and start playing with your toys. From time to time, turn round and ask him *'What are you doing?'* and show great interest in anything he shows or tells you. Comment that you are doing something very funny/different/clever. You hope that the child will ask what you are doing. If he doesn't, say 'Do you want to know what I'm doing?' and show him. Keep prompting him during the play session to ask what you are doing. You can do the same sort of thing with building bricks, Lego or modelling clay. You can also do it in the sandpit if you can find something to form a screen or barrier between you and the child.

6 **TEACHING TARGET: to use the question *What's this?***

▶ **Games**

A collection of small toys, box or bag

You need at least two children to make this game any fun. Tell the children you are going to see how quickly they can tell you the names of all the things in your box. Pull out the first toy and put it in front of a child, saying '*What's this?*' Encourage him to give you an answer. Pull out the next toy, put it in front of the second child, again saying '*What's this?*' Get the game going as fast as you can. When you have used up all the toys, put them back in the bag and let a child take over the 'teacher' role. Now he copies what you did and pulls out the toys one at a time, asking the other children in turn '*What's this?*'

7 **TEACHING TARGET: to use the question *What do you want?***

▶ **Home Corner**

Dolls, teddies, toy food, teaset

Extended play involving a tea party with big dolls, animals and teddies, and familiar foods from the toy food box. Follow the child's play for a while, then sit a doll, an animal and a teddy beside you and put the food items out on the table. Tell the child 'Teddy is hungry. What does he want to eat? You ask him.' If necessary, model the question for the child: '*What do you want*, Teddy? Oh, an apple. Here you are.' Give the teddy an apple and then point to the toy again. Suggest to the child again that he asks what the toy wants. Say '*What do you want*, Teddy?' Make the toy answer and supply the item it wants. Continue until all the food items are used up. Accept incomplete sentences at this stage ('*What want*, Teddy? *You want*, Teddy?), but continue to model the correct form after the child has asked his question. (eg child says '*What want*, Teddy?' and you repeat '*What do you want*, Teddy?' before giving the answer).

ASKING QUESTIONS
STAGE TWO

ACTIVITY AREAS ▶

▶ Songs & rhymes
▶ Picture books
▶ Construction & craft

▶ Hall/PE
▶ Games

QUESTION TYPES

Where is/are/was ...?

Where (do we, do I, does it ...?

Where shall I/we ...?

Where have I/you...?

Which (one ...)?

Which (way...)?

WHAT TO DO

Work through the *where*? activities in the order given. Plan as many more activities as you can for each question type before going on to the next, using ideas based on the examples.

• Move on to *which?* questions when you think *where?* is established.

• In all these activities it's a great help to include one or two children with good language skills, so that the child hears the modelled form of words lots of times.

TEACHING IDEAS

1 **TEACHING TARGET: to use the question *Where is? (Where's?)***

▶ **Songs & rhymes**

Toy sheep and cow, little boy, musical instrument

Teach the children the nursery rhyme 'Little Boy Blue' (Resources, p225). Have as many props as you can to illustrate it with – a picture of Little Boy Blue, a toy sheep, a toy cow and some sort of musical instrument to represent the horn. When the children are familiar with the words, encourage them to join in, particularly with '*Where's* the boy who looks after the sheep?'

2 **TEACHING TARGET: to use *Where have you?***

▶ **Songs & rhymes**

Toy cat

Teach the children the rhyme 'Pussy cat, pussy cat, where have you been?' (Resources, p226). Have a toy cat to illustrate it with. Once the children are familiar with the words, encourage them to join in, particularly in saying loudly to the cat '*Where have you been*?'

3 **TEACHING TARGET: to use the question *Where is? (Where's?)***

▶ **Hall**

A small toy for each child playing

Show the children 'their' toys and explain that later on you are going to hide them somewhere in the hall. Hide the toys so that they can't be seen easily, but so that the hiding places are accessible to the children.

When the time comes for the activity, set the children off around the hall to try and find 'their' toy. Give them individually some ideas as to where to look ('behind the curtains', 'under a bench', for example) and encourage them to come back to you if they fail to find the toy and ask you again either 'Where is it?' or 'Where shall I look?' Prompt the question if necessary, and encourage the child to use a correct sentence.

4 **TEACHING TARGET: to use the question *Where is? (Where's?)***

▶ **Picture books**

 A book with busy scenes or lots of different objects

Share the book with the child. You choose a picture to start with, and ask the child to find the things you name. ('*Where's* the bus? *Where's* the boy riding a bicycle? *Where's* the buggy?') You need to tailor your questions to the level of the child's vocabulary. Then let him choose a page and ask you to find things. Sometimes pretend to be having difficulty finding the object, so that the child can show you.

5 **TEACHING TARGET: to use the question *Where does?***

▶ **Games**

 A large floor puzzle

Everyone helps to put the puzzle together. Pretend to be stuck from time to time as to where to put the piece in your hand and ask '*Where does* this bit go?' Encourage the children to ask you or each other '*Where does* this bit go?'

6 **TEACHING TARGET: to use the questions *Where shall I?, Where do I?***

▶ **Construction & craft**

 Make two large simple identical drawings (eg house, animal, person), dividing them up rather like a jigsaw. Colour or paint one of the pictures, colouring the sections with different colours with a random pattern.

Give the child the uncoloured picture. Hand him different coloured pencils or paint pots one at a time for him to colour or paint one section. When he shows uncertainty as to where to colour, prompt him to ask '*Where shall I colour?*' or '*Where do I?*' When he's finished, show him that his picture matches yours. If your picture is big enough, you can do this activity with more than one child.

7 **TEACHING TARGET: to use the question *Which (one)?***

▶ **Construction & craft**

Leaves, flowers, twigs, fabric, paper, glue

A joint venture to make a big collage, sticking on leaves, flowers, twigs, pieces of material. Holding two different things one in each hand, offer the child a choice: '*Which one* do you want?' or '*Which* would you like?' When it is your turn to add something to the collage, a child gives you the choice. Show him that he can pick up any two things he likes and ask you '*Which one* do you want?' Prompt by saying 'Ask me.' Accept any question form that includes the word *which?* ('*Which* you want?' or just '*Which?*' or '*Which one?*') You can do the same activity with a collaborative painting project, this time offering the choice between two colours ('*Which* do you want – red or blue?')

8 **TEACHING TARGET: to use the question *Which way?***

▶ **Hall/PE**

A small 'assault course' set up in the hall (eg a bench to balance along, something to crawl under, a tunnel to crawl through, something to go round or between)

You need two or three children for this activity. Lead your team of followers round the course once. Then say 'Now let's go round the other way' and repeat the circuit. Now choose a child to be 'leader', but before he sets off say 'Just a minute! You don't know *which way* round to go.' If he looks blank or can't ask, prompt with 'Ask me *which way*.' When the child has led his team round, make one or two minor changes to the assault course, choose another child as leader, and repeat the performance.

ASKING QUESTIONS
STAGE THREE

ACTIVITY AREAS

- ▶ Games
- ▶ Circle games
- ▶ Storybooks
- ▶ Construction & craft
- ▶ Tabletop games

QUESTION TYPES

Who?

Why?

When?

WHAT TO DO

These question words are generally learnt in the order given in the box, so start with *Who?* and get that securely learnt before moving on.

- Before starting to teach the use of any of the words, check to see that the child understands what it means. It is fairly easy to do this with *who?* (eg in Circle Time ask who has got a red jumper on, who wants to be milk monitor, and so on). With the *why?* and *when?* words you can really only do it by observation, as the child is unlikely to be able to respond adequately.

- Work your way through the suggestions given. You will probably need to repeat some of them and to plan further activities based on the examples to consolidate learning.

TEACHING IDEAS

1 **TEACHING TARGET: to ask *Who?* questions**

▶ **Circle games**

A photo of each child as a baby

For this game you need to involve a group, the more the merrier. Ask the children to bring you in a photograph of themselves as a baby or toddler. Before they hand their photograph over to you, make sure they have had a good look at it and will recognise it again! Put the photographs in a box. Start the game off yourself by taking out one of the photographs, holding it up, and asking '*Who's* this?' When you have identified two or three photographs, get the child to take your place as 'teacher' and ask the questions. Encourage and prompt as necessary. If the child is shy about asking questions to a whole group, get a more confident child to have a turn ahead of him. This activity makes a good starting point for all sorts of further talking activities (growing up, family resemblances, present and previous homes, holidays if some are shown in any of the photographs).

2 **TEACHING TARGET: to ask *Who?* questions**

▶ **Tabletop games**

Picture Lotto

A game for at least four children, and a variation on the standard game (Resources, p220). One child takes the role of 'teacher' and has the baseboard and the pictures are distributed among the remaining children. The aim of the 'teacher' is to collect all the pictures one at a time, and complete the lotto board. You may need to start him off. Decide which picture you want first, and ask '*Who's* got the ...?' It is handed over, you place it on the board, and then ask for the next picture. When the children have got the idea, appoint each child in turn to be 'teacher'.

3 **TEACHING TARGET: to ask *Who?* questions**

▶ **Storybooks**

The story of *Goldilocks and the Three Bears* (Resources, p262)

Read the story of *Goldilocks and the Three Bears*, if necessary several times on different days. Once the child is familiar with the story, use the cloze procedure (Resources, p228). Read the story, and when you come to the moments where one of the bears asks '*Who's* been eating my porridge' (or sitting on my chair, or sleeping on my bed), stop reading, pause expectantly and wait for the child to fill in the words.

4 TEACHING TARGET: to ask *Why?* questions

▶ **Tabletop games**

A collection of action pictures or Why Because Cards (Resources, p263).

Why Because cards are packs of paired pictures. One picture shows, for example, a child covered in mud, while the second picture shows him playing football. Hold up a card and tell the child what is happening in the picture. ('This man looks very frightened.' 'This boy is crying.' 'This man is running very fast.' 'This boy is all muddy.') Prompt the child each time to ask '*Why?*' and then either show him the 'Because' card or if you are using individual pictures draw on your imagination to supply a reason. This is a good introductory game to the use of *Why?*

5 TEACHING TARGET: to ask *Why?* questions

▶ **Tabletop games**

Pictures to prompt the question *why?* Some ideas: somebody wearing a lot of cold-weather clothes, somebody wearing soaking wet clothes, somebody carrying a ladder, somebody climbing over a wall, somebody making a phone call, somebody going in to a toyshop

This activity is similar to the previous one, but instead of simple action pictures you need some carefully chosen pictures that prompt the child to ask full questions in language that is not too difficult. Show the child the pictures one at a time, and prompt him to ask questions like '*Why* has he got lots of clothes on?' '*Why* is he all wet?' '*Why* has he got a ladder?' You don't need to insist on correct grammar or every word being present, as long as there is a reasonable attempt to get his ideas across. Model the sentence for him afterwards using his own words (eg child says '*Why* he's all wet?' and you model '*Why is he* all wet? Because he fell in a pond.')

6 TEACHING TARGET: to ask *Why?* questions

▶ **Circle games**

Action pictures showing everyday routines such as brushing hair, brushing teeth, washing, dressing, sleeping, eating, drinking, exercising (see Resources, p263)

This game is harder. Explain that you are going to show the children pictures of things that we do every day. They have to ask '*Why?*' we need to do these things. Show a picture in turn to each child, but give no prompts except perhaps for the first one. This is a game where it is useful to have one or two linguistically competent children in the group to model the sort of sentences you are after (eg a picture of brushing hair – child asks '*Why* do we brush our hair?' or '*Why* do we have to brush our hair?).

7   **TEACHING TARGET: to use *When?* questions**

▶ **Construction & craft**

Special Calendar (Activity Sheet 7, Resources, pp243–5)

Identify two or three pleasant or unusual events that are going to take place during the week. If no pictures exist for them, help the child make appropriate stick-on pictures. Then get the calendar, tell the child 'Right, so the Life Caravan is coming. Shall we see *when*?' Prompt the child to ask '*When?*' or '*When* is it coming?' and help him stick the picture in the right place on the calendar. ('It's coming on Wednesday.') Do this with any other pictures of forthcoming special events for the week, and repeat in ensuing weeks. Increasingly prompt for full sentences.

8   **TEACHING TARGET: to ask *When?* questions**

▶ **Circle games**

A simple made-up story that children can ask *When?* questions about, pencil and paper

Read the story events out to the children one at a time. The children take turns to ask '*When*?' each event happened. You can either think of answers yourself, or get the children to discuss and decide when certain events took place. Jot down the final answers as you go along. At the end, retell the story including all the answers to the '*when?*' questions (eg Adult: 'Barney the Bear woke up.' Child 1: '*When* did he wake up?' Adult: 'Very early in the morning. It was his birthday.' Child 2 : '*When* was his birthday?' Adult: 'On May 3rd. He was very excited because he was going to have a party.' Child 3: '*When* was he going to have a party?' and so on.) Talk to the children about how important it is to a story to know *when* things happened.

9   **TEACHING TARGET: to use *When?* questions**

▶ **Circle games**

A list of the children's birthdays

Go round the circle. Each child asks his next door neighbour either '*When* will you be 5/6?' or '*When* will it be your birthday?' Prompt as necessary. Use the occasion to talk about summer/spring/autumn/winter birthdays, who is older than whom, things that happen on birthdays. Because you have the list of dates by you, you can help by pointing out for instance that somebody has just had his birthday. *When* was it? What happened?

ASKING QUESTIONS
STAGE FOUR

 **ACTIVITY AREAS**

▶ Music
▶ Cooking
▶ Circle games

▶ Construction & craft
▶ Tabletop games
▶ Reference books

QUESTION TYPES

How tall /many/often/much?

How do ...?

How does ...?

How can you tell?

WHAT TO DO

Leave *how often?* and *how can you tell?* questions till last.

- Where possible, teach all these *how?* questions in small groups, so that the child hears several other people asking the question before he has a turn. Include some children with good language skills if you can as models.

- Work your way through the teaching suggestions, adding more ideas of your own based on the examples.

TEACHING IDEAS

1 **TEACHING TARGET: to ask *How tall?* questions**

▶ **Construction & craft**

Lego or bricks, measuring tape or pole

Give the children a few minutes in which to make towers of Lego or bricks. When they have finished, tell them you want to find out how tall their towers are. Ask the first child: '*How tall* is your tower?' and help him to measure it. Unless you want this to be part of a numeracy activity, don't worry about whether the child can actually get the height right, just check and record it for him. Then encourage him to ask another child '*How tall* is your tower?' or '*How tall* is yours?' Record all the heights and at the end let the children arrange their towers in height order. As a further activity you could let the children measure each other's height, length of arms, and so on. This type of activity can be used to teach lots of other *how?* questions (eg *how* big?, *how* long?, *how* heavy?, *how* wide?)

2 **TEACHING TARGET: to ask *How many?/How much?* questions**

▶ **Cooking**

Ingredients for basic biscuits, scales, baking sheet, large bowl, spoon, rolling pin

A cooking activity for three or four children. Rather than telling the children what to do at each step, give the minimum of information so that they need to ask for more help. For instance start by saying 'You need flour in the bowl.' Prompt the question '*How much?*' before helping as usual with the measuring. Do the same with further ingredients. ('You need some butter.' '*How much?*' 'Now some egg/milk/currants' – prompting the questions '*How many?*' '*How much?*') Make sure that the child gets plenty of turns at asking. Before cutting out the biscuit shapes, get the children to guess how many biscuits the dough will make. Encourage them to answer by saying '*How many* do I think? I think …'

3 **TEACHING TARGET: to ask *How do you/I?* questions**

▶ **Music**

As many musical instruments as you can assemble

Encourage the children to handle the various instruments. Tell them the names of the instruments. Then let each child choose one instrument, and in turn ask you '*How do you* play it?' Model the question if necessary. Demonstrate what to do with each instrument, and accept help from any child who already knows. Let the children try them out as far as is practicable, as in the course of this more *how?* questions will crop up. ('*How do I* put my fingers? *How do I* hold the bow? *How* hard *do* I blow?')

(4) **TEACHING TARGET: to ask *How does?* questions**

▶ **Reference books**

Book showing pictures of tools and machines (eg hammer, pliers, screwdriver, augur, plane, clamp, car jack, crane)

Show a picture to each child in turn and let them take turns to ask '*How does* it work?' Model the question for the first child if necessary. Enlist the help of any children who know some of the answers. If you can find individual pictures of the tools and machines this is easier, as the children can have a picture each.

(5) **TEACHING TARGET: to ask *How often?* questions**

▶ **Construction & craft**

Special Calendar and its detachable pictures (Activity Sheet 7, Resources, pp243–5) covering several weeks

Get the Special Calendar down from its place and put it on the table. Take off all the stick-on pictures. Tell the children you are going to find out *how often* things happen – like Assembly, PE, Cooking, Swimming, Playtime, visits from the Music Teacher, and so on. Let the children take turns to identify an activity and prompt the question '*How often* do we have Assembly? *How often* does the Music Teacher come?' If the child gives a slightly incorrect sentence (eg '*How often we do have*' or '*How often do* the Music Teacher come?'), accept it, but re-model the correct version before talking about the answer. Help the children re-attach the pictures and count up how often the various events occur, either over a week or over a period of several weeks.

(6) **TEACHING TARGET: to ask *How can you tell?* questions**

▶ **Circle games**

Slips of paper with some scenarios written on them

Examples of scenarios: How can you tell there is a monster in the cupboard, someone has walked through the snow, there is someone at the door, the car has been for a drive, it's been raining, your friend is sleepy, your Gran is going on holiday, Uncle Jim is going to play football? Give each child a slip and when it is their turn prompt them to ask '*How can you tell…?*' and read out their slip for them. If you haven't included children with reasonable language skills in your group, you may have to come up with suggestions yourself. (Answers might be: 'You can hear horrible growling.' 'There are footprints.' 'You can hear knocking.' 'The engine is hot.')

USING GRAMMAR
STAGE TWO

ACTIVITY AREAS

▶ Small toy play
▶ Pictures

Plural /s/

WHAT TO DO

First check whether the child can hear and understand the difference between the words (eg 'cat' and 'cats', 'horse' and 'horses'). Does he know that 'cat' means one cat, while 'cats' means two or more? If he doesn't, teaching will have to begin at the level of understanding the concept. Get out the farm animals. Put one cat or one cow on its own, and two or more cats or two or more cows a little way away. Ask the child to show you the cat – the cats – the cows – the cow. Can he do it?

- Next check whether the child can pronounce the sound /s/. Make a long hissing 'snake' sound. Can the child copy you? Does he use the /s/ sound in his everyday speech? If the answer to either of these is no, this grammar target will have to wait until he has been taught or spontaneously acquired the /s/ sound.

- Start teaching with the words that take just /s/ as their plural (eg cats, cars, cows, hats, coats, boats, hens, boys, girls, cups). Only when the child is using these reliably move on to the second group (horses, buses, races, houses, faces).

- Use these teaching ideas, with modifications where necessary, *in the order given.*

TEACHING IDEAS

1 **TEACHING TARGET: to associate the toy snake with the sound '*sssss*'**

▶ **Small toy play**

 Small toy animals, a toy snake (glove puppet, toy or made of playdough), counters

First, put out all the toy animals on the table or floor. Go through them with the child, making sure he knows what sound each animal makes, and that he can make the sounds himself. Make a special point of teaching him that the snake goes 'sssss', a long hissing sound. Now hide the snake in your lap. Tell the child that you are going to point to the animals in turn and he has got to make their sound. Every so often the snake will pop up and the child must remember to make his hissing noise. When he gets it right he gets a counter.

2 **TEACHING TARGET: to start putting a /s/ on the end of plural words**

▶ **Small toy play**

 Small toys from the farm and doll's house, the toy snake

Get the child to help you put out the toys, grouped in ones, twos or more (eg one cup on its own, two or three cups together, one cat on its own, a group of cats). Point to a single toy, for example a cup, and say 'One cup' or 'A cup'. Then point to the group of cups and say 'Two cups' or 'Three cups' or 'Lots of cups'. Emphasise the /s/ sound, holding up the snake as you do so. Remind the child that the /s/ on the end means there's more than one. Now it's the child's turn. Help and prompt him to name the single and grouped objects, holding up the snake each time as a reminder to put the /s/ on when appropriate. The first time you try this, point to the cup and cups, boat and boats as contrasting pairs. Later on, do them in random order: a cup, some boats, a boat, two cats.

3 **TEACHING TARGET: to put the /s/ on plural words without prompting**

▶ **Pictures**

 Set of 'Plural' pictures (Resources, p250), toy snake

Use the Teddy Game pictures (except 'glasses') to make a set of single items and a set of pairs of the same items, eg two apples, etc. Take turns with the child to pick up the pictures in random order, saying what is in the picture (for example 'A boat', 'Two cups, etc). Use the snake as a reminder when necessary. Once the child can do this task with reasonable success, teachers and teaching assistants should be alerted to give gentle reminders when the child forgets his plurals in everyday speech.

4 **TEACHING TARGET: to start using the *-es* plural ending**

▶ **Pictures**

You will need pictures of a horse, a bus, a mouse, a house, a face and a dish that can be made into cards with a) a single picture or b) two or more. For example, one bus/two buses.

This step can be left till several weeks after the child is using the plural /s/ reliably. Sort out the *-es* plural pictures, and make a pack of them in pairs (horse/horses, bus/buses). Take turns to pick up a card, naming the picture. Arrange things so that the child gets the single pictures and you get the groups. Emphasise the *-es* ending on your pictures. Now shuffle the pack and see if the child can remember to put the *-es* ending on where appropriate. Prompt and help as much as necessary. When he can do this task reliably, teachers and teaching assistants should be alerted to give gentle reminders when the child forgets his *-es* endings in everyday speech.

USING GRAMMAR
STAGE THREE

ACTIVITY AREAS
▶ Tabletop games
▶ Storybooks

Past tense -*ed*

WHAT TO DO

Check whether the child can hear and understand the difference between, for example, 'walk' and 'walk*ed*', or 'hop' and 'hopp*ed*'. Does he know that the little -*ed* sound on the end of some action words should be there when something happened in the past? Read a little story, with lots of -*ed* (regular) past tenses (eg 'Johnny woke early on Sunday. He jump*ed* out of bed, walk*ed* to the window, and look*ed* out. He call*ed* and whistl*ed*. Suddenly the tame robin hopp*ed* on to the windowsill, and peck*ed* at the seeds Johnny had put out for it.') Point out the significance of the -*ed* to the child. Then read the story again and sometimes say the action words wrongly (eg 'He jump out of bed', 'The tame robin hop on to the windowsill.'). Tell the child he has to spot when you are saying something wrong. Can he do it? If not, teaching has to begin at this level.

- Use the teaching ideas in the order given.

TEACHING IDEAS

1 **TEACHING TARGET: to be able to say words with -ed on the end**

▶ **Table top games**

Race Board (Activity Sheet 1, Resources, p233)

Play the game in the normal way. When the child lands on a star, say a past tense word for him to copy. If he gets it right he moves forward one space. If he gets it wrong he moves back a space. In some action words which take the regular past tense (walked, hopped, skipped), the -ed sounds like a /t/. In others, it sounds like a /d/ (cried, screamed, yelled).

2 **TEACHING TARGET: to be able to use the -ed past tense ending appropriately in response to a question**

▶ **Storybooks**

A suitable story with lots of past tense narrative

First read the story to the child once through. Point out some of the -ed words. Then read the story again, stopping as often as you can to ask 'What did he do?' or 'What happened?' Prompt and encourage the child to respond with a past tense action word (eg 'Mum cooked a big cake for Jake's birthday. What did Mum do?' Child responds: 'Cooked a cake.') Do this with different stories over a few weeks. Once the child can respond accurately without prompting, it is time to alert teachers and teaching assistants to give gentle reminders when the child forgets his -ed endings in everyday speech.

USING GRAMMAR
STAGE FOUR

ACTIVITY AREAS

- ▶ Storybooks
- ▶ Pencil & paper
- ▶ Games

IRREGULAR PAST TENSES

ran	flew	saw	bought
drew	swam	ate	drank
slept	threw	caught	thought
went	blew	knew	

IRREGULAR PLURALS

children	men	sheep	feet
teeth	women	leaves	geese

WHAT TO DO

These little bits of grammar can really only be taught by practice and repetition.

- Use the list of irregular past tenses and add others as necessary. Irregular past tenses are the ones that do not follow the *-ed* rule but have special past tense forms that may be unique to that action word.

- Make a note of the ones the child doesn't use.

- Teach not more than three irregular past tenses at a time. Some children can learn two or three at once, while others may need to be introduced to them singly.

- Teach each word or group of words using the teaching ideas in the order given. Only when the child can use a set of target words spontaneously should you move on to a new word or words.

- Do the irregular plurals later, after a few weeks' break. See the list above.

TEACHING IDEAS

1 TEACHING TARGET: to start recognising the correct past tense form of irregular verbs

▶ **Storybooks or made up stories**

A short story containing lots of repetition of the words you are targeting

Read the story through to the child. Point out the fact that some of the words are very special, and don't follow the usual rules. Read the story again, this time using the *-ed* form instead of the proper one. Can the child spot your 'mistakes'? (eg 'Jack swimmed across the pool' 'Jenny throwed some bread to the ducks.')

2 TEACHING TARGET: to be able to use target irregular past tenses in a structured situation

▶ **Storybooks or made up stories**

Use the same story used in Teaching Target 1

Read the story again, either using the cloze procedure (Resources, p228) for the child to fill in the target words, or asking questions such as 'What did he do?' or 'What happened?' (eg 'Jack swam across the pool. What did Jack do?' 'Jenny … some bread to the ducks.') You may sometimes need to mime the action to cue in the child. Prompt or correct as necessary.

3 TEACHING TARGET: to be able to use the target word or words spontaneously

▶ **Games**

Writing materials or tape recorder, a music player (optional)

Tell the child that it is his turn now to make up a story. Give him a subject that relates to the past tense(s) you have been working on, for example feeding the ducks. Start him off by saying 'Once upon a time …' to prompt him to tell the story in the past. Write down his story as he dictates it, or you might like to record it on a tape recorder. At the end, read the story back to him, or listen to it together on tape. Help him correct any mistakes over the irregular past tenses. When his use of a set of target words seems fairly secure, it is time to alert teachers and teaching assistants to give him gentle reminders when he forgets his 'new' words in everyday speech.

TALKING IN SENTENCES
STAGE ONE

ACTIVITY AREAS
- ▶ Songs & rhymes
- ▶ Circle games
- ▶ Hall/PE
- ▶ Games

- ▶ Sand & water
- ▶ Home Corner
- ▶ Construction & craft

WHAT TO DO

Stage One aims to teach a small selection of basic sentence types, and some ways of extending them. Plan as many additional activities as you can for every target, using ideas from the examples.

- Do not try to teach the child to use these sentences unless you are sure he understands them when you use them. Make sure he understands all the words involved.

- Don't expect him to manage every word in the longer sentences, just the key ones. Help, model and prompt as much as necessary – don't let him struggle.

TEACHING IDEAS

❶ TEACHING TARGET: to use two-element sentences (*brush hair, wash face*)

▶ **Songs & rhymes**

 A list of action words that are easy to carry out or mime

Play and sing 'Here We Go Round the Mulberry Bush' (Resources, p221). Once you have sung it once or twice, put the child in the middle of the circle. His job is to think of an action, and fill in the words as he mimes it (eg the group sings 'This is the way we …' and the child says and mimes 'wash our face/brush our hair/clap our hands', and so on). Help as necessary by either just miming an action as a prompt, or supplying the words if necessary.

2 **TEACHING TARGET: to use two-element sentences (*clap* your *hands*, *stamp* your *feet*)**

▶ **Songs & rhymes**

None

Sing or chant 'If You're Happy and You Know It' (Resources, p224). After one or two runs through, use the cloze procedure (Resources, p228) for the key bits, but continue to mime the actions to prompt the children to fill in the words. ('If you're happy and you know it *clap* your *hands*.') An even simpler action rhyme just goes 'Stamp your feet, stamp your feet, stamp, stamp, stamp. Clap your hands, clap your hands, clap, clap, clap. Wave your hand, wave your hand, wave, wave, wave', and so on.

3 **TEACHING TARGET: to use two-element sentences (*mix* a *pancake*, *stir* a *pancake*)**

▶ **Songs & rhymes**

Frying pan, bowl, spoon, pretend pancake of playdough or modelling clay

Say the 'Pancake Poem' (by Christina Rossetti, Resources, p226) letting the children mime the actions. Let the child learning the target use the props. Better still, do this activity in a cooking session, and make real pancakes. Once the children are familiar with the poem, use the cloze procedure for the key sentences ('*Mix* a *pancake*' '*Stir* a *pancake*') while you mime the actions.

4 **TEACHING TARGET: to use two-element sentences (*Susie, sit down*; *Tom, jump*)**

▶ **Circle games**

A picture book showing simple actions

Make sure the children all know each others' names. Play a variation of the Winking game. Explain to the children that you are going to show them a picture. Then you are going to wink at someone, and they have to do the action shown in the picture. It is useful to have another adult in the circle to demonstrate or help. When you have played the game more than once, select a child to be the 'teacher'. Give this child a picture of one of the actions. He has to tell somebody what to do ('*Susie, stand up.*' '*Jacob, lie down.*') Some examples of suitable action words: turn round, wave, smile, cry, sleep (go to sleep), clap, stamp, snore, cough, laugh, whisper, shout.

⑤ **TEACHING TARGET: to use two-element sentences (*Lucy hopped, Rashid jumped*)**

▶ **Hall/PE**

 None

A game for a group of six or more, or it could be played with the whole class. Stand all the children in a row facing a wall. Quietly select one child to carry out an action, and the child learning the target as your 'helper'. Tell the first child to hop/walk/run/dance/skip/jump across the room. Your helper then has to tell the rest of the group what happened. ('*Lucy hopped.*') If you get just half of the description – just the name of the child, or the name of the action, prompt for the other bit and then model the complete answer for the child. ('Well done. Lucy hopped. That's right.') Don't worry if the child's grammar is wrong and he says 'Lucy hop', or 'runned'. Send the rest of the children off to copy the action. Repeat with another pair of children and a different action. You could of course keep the same 'helper' throughout.

⑥ **TEACHING TARGET: to use sentences with two action words (*Go* and *look*)**

▶ **Games**

 A collection of small objects (eg car, cup, pencil, brush, book, miniature doll)

A Hunt-the-Thimble type game (Resources, p221). Put out the objects in front of the children and let them have a good look, so they will know what they are hunting for. Choose a 'hider'. Tell the rest of the children either to shut their eyes or, if they cannot do this reliably, to turn their backs, while the 'hider' takes one of the objects and hides it. When he is ready, he says '*Go* and *look*' (prompt him) and sends the 'searchers' off. Whoever finds the item brings it back, and either the same child hides another object or a different child is chosen. If an object is not found, the 'hider' goes to where it is and tells the other children to '*come* and *see*' (prompt him again with the words to use).

7 **TEACHING TARGET: to use a sentence with the word give and a person (*Give* the bag to *Sarah*)**

▶ **Circle games**

A beanbag

Choose a child as your 'helper'. Explain to the children that you are going to ask the person holding the beanbag some questions. Give the bag to your helper and tell him '*Give* the bag (or *give* it) to *Sarah*.' When Sarah is holding the bag, ask her a question (it might be 'How old are you? 'What colour is your jumper?' 'Where is your nose?' – tailor the question to the child's ability). Your 'helper' then decides who should receive the beanbag next and tells Sarah '*Give* it (or *give* the beanbag) to *George*.' Repeat until everyone has had a turn, either using the same helper if he is the child learning the target, or varying the helper from time to time.

8 **TEACHING TARGET: to use a sentence with 'I've got' and an object (*I've got* a car)**

▶ **Circle games**

An assortment of small toys and objects in a bag

Pass the bag round the circle. As each child receives the bag, he must take something out of it and tell what he has (eg '*I've got* a *car*.' '*I've got* a *spoon*.'). You can make this more fun by playing it to music like Pass the Parcel (Resources, p222). The child who is holding the bag when the music stops has to take out the object and say what he's got.

9 **TEACHING TARGET: to use some describing words in a phrase**

▶ **Sand & water**

Sandpit with some containers, buckets, spades, water, a few vehicles

Extended play. Join the child playing in the sandpit. Follow his play and at the same time introduce words like big/little, tall, wet/dry, heavy, sticky, fast ('I'm making a *big castle*. And here's a *little one*, look. This sand is too *dry* – I'll put some water on. Now it's nice and *sticky*' and so on). Encourage the child to comment on his play using some of these words ('That's a *big castle* – what are you making now?')

⑩ TEACHING TARGET: to use some describing words in a phrase

▶ **Home Corner**

Big dolls and teddies, teaset and cooking equipment, table and chairs, sink

Extended play. Join the child preparing some tea for the toys, feeding them and clearing up. Introduce the idea of a toy spilling his drink, getting food on his clothes, dropping bits on the floor. ('Oh dear, my teddy's spilt his juice. Now the *table's dirty – clumsy teddy*. Let's wipe it up – there we are, all *clean* again.') Encourage the child to imitate your play and comment in the same way. When it's time to clear up, offer the child plates, spoons, cups, etc. to 'wash up'. ('Is this plate *clean* or *dirty*? Oh, *a dirty plate*. Here you are – wash it up.')

⑪ TEACHING TARGET: to use words indicating ownership (*my, Robert's*)

▶ **Hall/PE**

None

Do this activity in preparation for any simple team game. Appoint the child as a team leader. He has the chance to choose the members of his own and the other child's team. He must point to each child and say '*My* team' or '*Robert's* team'. You may have to intervene and help if one team is getting out of proportion.

⑫ TEACHING TARGET: to use *again* and *more*

▶ **Sand & water**

Containers, buckets, spades, some vehicles

Extended play. Join the child in building castles, pouring water, driving vehicles. Do some things that he has not thought of or can't manage – making a perfect castle by filling your bucket to the brim and tipping it out, or pouring the sand or water into the waterwheel. Encourage him to ask you to do it *again* (prompt with 'Say "Do it again".').

Prompt the use of *more* in any everyday activity eg. *more* juice or water at snack time, *more* paint at painting time, *more* music at band time.(Tell the child: 'Say "More paint please".')

⑬ TEACHING TARGET: to use *in/on/under* in a phrase

▶ **Construction & craft**

A picture drawn on a really big piece of paper of a house, tree, table, bed, box, car (or any other items that can be used to place other objects on, in or under)

Seat the children where they can see your picture clearly. Tell them you want to put some more things in the picture, and you need their help to know where to put them. Suggest, for example: 'I want to put a bird *in*. Where shall I put it?' If the children want to give funny answers, like '*in the box*' or '*under the bed*' that's fine. Put in the bird as instructed. Then say, for example, 'Now I want to put a rabbit *in*.' Carry on in this way until your picture is full, and everyone has had a turn or several turns. Model the *in/on/under* phrases for the children at first if necessary.

⑭ TEACHING TARGET: to use *in/on/under* in a phrase

▶ **Hall/PE**

Small toys or objects, box or bag

An activity for a small group. Take the child who is learning the target with you to the hall and hide several small toys or objects around the room. Help him put some of them *on* a bench, a table, or chair; some of them *under* a piece of furniture or a mat; some of them *in* a box or bag. Talk to the child about where you are putting things: 'Let's put the car *on* this table. Let's put the horse *in* this box.' Note how many things you have hidden. When the rest of the group come in, explain that they are going on a treasure hunt. The child has to tell them where to look. They can either be sent off one at a time to find an object, or can all search at once, depending on the size of the group. Prompt the child to tell them '*In the box*' or '*Under the mat*', and if he can manage it '*Look in the box/ under the mat.*' When the children think they have found everything, compare with the number you hid. See if anyone can find the missing items and tell where they were hidden.

TALKING IN SENTENCES
STAGE TWO

ACTIVITY AREAS

- ► Small toy play
- ► Home Corner
- ► Picture books
- ► Hall/PE

WHAT TO DO

Stage Two aims to extend the range of basic sentence types. Plan as many additional activities as you can for every target, using ideas from the examples.

- Do not try to teach the child to use these sentences unless you are sure he understands them when *you* use them. Make sure he understands all the words involved.

- Don't expect him to manage every word in the longer sentences, just the key ones. Help, model and prompt as much as necessary – don't let him struggle.

TEACHING IDEAS

1 **TEACHING TARGET: to use three-element sentences including position**

► **Small toy play**

 Toy farm and farm animals, vehicles, toy people

Extended play. Join the child in setting out the farm. Comment on your own play using sentences like: 'This *cow's going in the field'* 'The *tractor's driving on the road'* 'The *pigs are walking into the barn'*. Prompt the child to comment similarly by asking 'What's happening over there?' and 'What's that man doing?' Accept any attempt to tell you. Then model a good sentence back to the child: 'Oh yes – the cows are going in the field' or 'I see – he's driving on the road.' Keep the language natural. The child's comments do not have to conform to exact patterns. If he introduces other position words (eg do*wn, into, up, to)* so much the better. Don't worry if he leaves out non-essential words (eg 'Cows going in field' or 'Man driving on road').

2 **TEACHING TARGET: to use a three-element sentence including position**

▶ **Songs & rhymes**

A toy monkey and boy, bed

Sing or chant 'Five little Monkeys' (Resources, p224). Demonstrate with your toy monkey. Once the child knows the rhyme, use the cloze procedure (Resources, p228) to prompt him to say '*jumping on the bed'*. If he manages that, see if he can do '*monkeys jumping on the bed'*.

3 **TEACHING TARGET: to use three-element sentences**

▶ **Picture books**

A picture book showing lots of activities, eg a *girl riding* a *bike*, a *dog eating* his *dinner*, a *boy kicking* a *ball*, a *man driving* a *car*

Take turns with the child to find a picture and say what is happening. You start off, modelling the kind of sentence you want. Then identify a suitable picture for the child. Prompt him if necessary: 'What/who is it? A boy or a girl? What's he doing? He's kicking a …'. When the child has had a good try, model the sentence for him: 'That's right – it's a *boy kicking* a *ball*.' You can do this activity as a circle game too, including some children with good language skills. If the child is successful, you can aim to include a describing word as well: 'a *boy riding* a *big bike*' or 'a *man driving* a *blue car*'. Be aware that at this stage many children don't know their colours.

4 **TEACHING TARGET: to use describing words in a sentence**

▶ **Hall/PE**

Some big and little balls, in a box or container

Stand the children in a circle, with the box of balls in the middle. Bring a pair of children into the middle. One is the 'instructor', the other does what he is told. The instructor can choose to say, for example, '*Throw* a *big ball* to *Jack'* or '*Throw* a *little ball* to *Kirsty.'* The named child catches the ball, throws it back and replaces one of the children in the middle of the circle. Make sure the child learning the target gets several turns at being the 'instructor'.

5 **TEACHING TARGET: to use describing words in a sentence**

▶ **Small toy play**

 Trains and train track, or vehicles and playmat

Extended play. Join the child driving the trains round the track, or the cars and lorries round the roads on the playmat. Enlarge on the child's comments. For example, the child says 'My car's going on the road.' You say 'Yes, you've got the racing car/blue car/fast car, haven't you? Your blue car's going on the road.'

Be aware that many children at this stage don't know their colours.

6 **TEACHING TARGET: to use sentences involving ownership.**

▶ **Small toy play**

 Doll's house and miniature dolls

Extended play. Join the child in arranging the furniture and people in the doll's house. Talk about Mummy's bed and chair, Daddy's bed and chair, baby's cot/high chair. ('Mummy's bed is going in here. Let's put this doll in Mummy's bed.') Prompt the child to tell you where he is putting things: 'Is that Daddy's bed or Mummy's bed? Where does it go? Shall we put Daddy's car outside here?'

TALKING IN SENTENCES
STAGE THREE

ACTIVITY AREAS
- ▶ Circle games
- ▶ Small toy play
- ▶ Games
- ▶ Storybooks
- ▶ Construction & craft
- ▶ Tabletop games

Sentences of 4–5 words +

Sentences linked by *and*

WHAT TO DO

Make sure you don't attempt to teach sentences that are too hard for the child to understand.

- Work your way through the activities in any order. Plan additional activities using ideas from the examples given.

- Don't try to teach the child to link sentences with *and* if he doesn't already link *words* with *and* (eg 'I got a bucket *and* spade, I can see Mummy *and* Daddy.') You can use circle games to teach that level. Pass round a bag containing all sorts of small toys and prompt the children to take out one toy at a time saying: 'There's a car – and a tractor – and a man – and a dog' and so on.

TEACHING IDEAS

1 **TEACHING TARGET: to link sentences with *and***

▶ **Circle games**

None

Talk to the children about what they do every school morning. Discuss what they have for breakfast, differences in routine, how they get to school. Then start a sequence round the circle. Prompt the first child to say 'In the morning I get up.' The next child should continue '*and* I get dressed'. The next child adds '*and* I go downstairs'. Allow for any amount of variation in the order in which the children do things, but point it out if they miss something vital such as 'I go to school' before 'I get dressed'. Prompt as necessary, emphasising the *and*. Keep the narrative going as long as they can.

2 **TEACHING TARGET: to give an instruction involving description and position**

▶ **Small toy play**

Toy farm with animals, people, buildings, fields and fences, pond, etc (adapted to the child's preferences such as train set, doll's house)

Tell the child you are going to take turns to be the teacher. First you will tell him where to put something (eg 'Put a cow behind the barn/put the man on the tractor/ put a horse in the field.') When he has done as you ask, it's his turn to tell you what to do. Prompt him if necessary by asking: 'What do you want me to get? Where shall I put it? Tell me all of it again.' Take turns in this way until the child is using this kind of sentence confidently. (Position words to use: *in/on/under/ behind/in front*, and possibly *up on/by*)

Do this activity again on another occasion. This time include choices (eg 'Put the *black* horse in the field. Put the *big* tractor by the house. Put the *white* cow behind the tree.') Each time it is the child's turn to tell you what to do, prompt him by asking questions as before. ('Which horse shall I get? The black one or the white one? Where shall I put it? Tell me all of it again.') Try as far as possible to end up doing what the child actually wanted you to do.

3 **TEACHING TARGET: to use a sentence including a descriptive phrase**

▶ **Games**

Teddy pictures (Activity Sheet 9, Resources, pp248–50), photocopied and cut out

Have a look at the pictures with the child, and talk about them. 'Look, this teddy's got a hat. And here's a teddy with a car.' Then play Hunt the Picture. Hide the pictures around the room and ask the child to go and find them. He should bring each one back to you as he finds it. Ask him which teddy he has found. ('*One with* a *hat*? A *teddy with* a *car*? A *teddy with* an *ice-cream*? A *teddy with boots*?') Prompt him to tell you using all the key words. You can extend this game by enlarging a set of object pictures. Now the child will have to tell whether he has 'a teddy with *big* boots,' 'a teddy with a *little* car', 'a teddy with a big hat on'. If the child knows his colours, you can extend this activity still further by colouring in some of the pictures. Now the child will have to tell you he has found 'a teddy with a *big green* hat', 'a teddy with *little red* boots'.

4 **TEACHING TARGET: to use a sentence with two main action words**

▶ **Games**

Toys

Hide some toys around the room. They need to be visible without having to move anything. Jot down a list of what's hidden where. Send the children off to search one at a time. When a child sees a toy he mustn't collect it, but must come back and tell you and the other children what he has seen. Prompt for sentences like 'I know what's on top of the cupboard.' 'I saw what's hiding behind the curtain.' 'I know what you put under the table.' 'I've found the car you put in the box.' You won't always get the sentence you are aiming for, but accept what's offered. When everyone has had a turn, send them off again one at a time saying, '*Get* the car I *put* on top of the cupboard.' '*Find* the train I *hid* in the box.' Your sentences should always include *get/fetch/find* or *bring*, and *put* or *hid*.

5 **TEACHING TARGET: to use a sentence with two main action words**

▶ **Circle games**

A large soft toy, doll or puppet

You have the toy to start with. Say to the children: '*Watch* Teddy *jump* up and down' or '*Watch* Teddy *go to sleep*' or '*Watch* Teddy *turn round* and round'. Then hand the toy to a child. Prompt him to think what he is going to make Teddy do. Then prompt him to say '*Watch* Teddy ...' which you can reinforce if you see somebody who is not watching. ('Look, Jessica's not watching. Don't forget to tell her to *watch* Teddy.') Let the children's imagination run riot over what to make Teddy do.

6 **TEACHING TARGET: to use a sentence with strings of ideas**

▶ **Circle games**

 None

Tell the children you are going to play a game where you keep thinking of ideas for as long as you can. Start them off with, for example, 'I'm thinking of a bear who's big and ...' Point to each child in turn for a contribution (eg black – and hairy – and cross –). When the list of describing words dries up, prompt with 'and he likes to eat buns and ...' (see if you can get a list of foods, however ridiculous). When that dries up, prompt with 'and he lives in a cave which is ... (dark, smelly, big, wet, etc). This game is purely to give the children an idea of the fun that can be had with words.

7 **TEACHING TARGET: to retell short bits of a familiar story**

▶ **Storybooks**

 A popular story with vocabulary and language within the child's ability (stories with lots of repetition, particularly little repetitive rhymes, are especially good)

Read the story to the child on two or three occasions, sharing the pictures. Next time you read it, use the cloze procedure (Resources, p228) to prompt him to produce a key phrase or sentence. Gradually extend the number of words you want him to remember and say. (Example: *The Gingerbread Man* (Resources, p262). When you get to the little rhyme, read 'Run, run, as fast as you can, you can't catch me, I'm ...'. If the child finds it easy to complete the rhyme, try 'Run, run, as fast as you can, you can't catch me ...' and so on.)

TALKING IN SENTENCES
STAGE FOUR

ACTIVITY AREAS

- ▶ Games
- ▶ Construction & craft
- ▶ Hall/PE
- ▶ Pencil & paper
- ▶ Music

SENTENCES USING

but	because
so	or
if	when

WHAT TO DO

Do not try to teach the child to use these words in sentences unless you are sure he understands them when you use them.

- You will have to model these sentences (Resources, p229) before expecting the child to be able to produce them himself.

- Make sure he knows any other vocabulary such as the names of items in the pictures.

- Do not let him struggle with a sentence – help out immediately he gets stuck.

TEACHING IDEAS

① **TEACHING TARGET: to say a sentence containing *but***

▶ **Hall/PE**

 Four different coloured hoops and matching beanbags

This is a game for up to four children. Lay the hoops on the floor, well spaced. Put a beanbag in each hoop. Explain to the children that the beanbags are 'monsters' and must not be touched. Then give each child a short simple instruction as follows: 'Stand in the blue hoop, *but* don't touch the monster. Sit in the red hoop, *but* don't touch the monster.' Give each child a practice turn, then choose a child to give the instruction, using your model. If the child learning the target cannot manage the whole sentence, try saying the first bit for him and seeing if he can finish it. Alternatively, give the instruction together, until he can do it himself.

② **TEACHING TARGET: to finish a sentence using *but***

▶ **Storybooks**

 The story of *Goldilocks and the Three Bears* (Resources, p262)

Read the story to the child more than once if he is not familiar with it. Then go through the story again, encouraging the child to finish some of the sentences. For example, 'She tried the first bowl of porridge' (child says '*but* it was too hot'). '*She tried Mummy Bear's bed*' (child says '*but* it was too soft').

③ **TEACHING TARGET: to say sentences using *because***

▶ **Games – Fairy Tale game**

 Race Board, Situation Cards (Activity Sheets 1 and 11, Resources, pp233 and 252), counters and a die

To play the Fairy Tale Game, roll the die and when a player lands on a star they take a card from the pile. Ask the question on the card. The child must start his answer with '*Because …*'. Example: 'Why was Cinderella sad?' '*Because* she couldn't go to the ball.' They must be stories the child knows. To start with you may have to model the answers. Give as much help as the child needs. It will probably take several attempts before he succeeds. You can make further sets of cards based on stories the child is familiar with.

4 **TEACHING TARGET: to say *because* in a sentence**

▶ **Circle games**

A copy of the *Why?* questions (Activity Sheet 10, Resources, p251)

Go round the circle asking each child a question from your sheet. The answers should begin '*Because*'. Model the answer first and say it in unison with the child for the first few attempts. Accept muddled sentences as long as they include 'because'.

5 **TEACHING TARGET: to use *so* in a sentence**

▶ **Storybooks**

The story of *The Very Hungry Caterpillar* (Resources, p261)

Read the story to the child several times so that he is really familiar with it. Then go through it modelling the target phrase '*so he ate a ...*'. Encourage the child to join in the target phrase with you. Then go through it again, this time letting the child say the target phrase on his own. You will have to revisit the story over several days.

6 **TEACHING TARGET: to use *so* in a sentence**

▶ **Small toy play**

Toy farm and animals

You are going to make up a simple story, using the farm animals as props. The child will say parts of the story, using the target phrase, as you move the animals accordingly. Example: 'The pig was in his field. The farmer left the gate open.' (Now make the pig leave the field and model the sentence, '*So* he went out through the gate.') 'The cow saw that the pig had got out of the field. His gate was shut.' (Now make the cow jump over the fence and model the target phrase, '*So* he jumped over the fence.') 'The cow and the pig saw a big pile of hay near the tractor.' (Make them eat the hay and encourage the child to say the target phrase, '*So* they went and ate it all up'.) Now repeat the sequence again, this time letting the child say the target phrases. Once he has got it you can continue with another similar sequence.

7 **TEACHING TARGET: to use *or* in a sentence**

▶ **Games**

A collection of small items to buy

This is most fun played with a small group. The child learning the target is the shopkeeper. Give him a pair of items. Make sure he knows what they are called. The first child comes to the shop and the 'shopkeeper' says, for example, 'Do you want the pencil *or* the book?' You may have to model the sentence first. Give him the next pair of items and continue in the same way.

8 **TEACHING TARGET: to use *or* in a sentence**

▶ **Construction & craft**

Simple line drawings of familiar objects, two different colours of paint, two brushes

The child is going to ask the adult or another child which colour they would like to paint each of the drawings. Start by modelling the sentence. Give the child a picture and ask 'Do you want red *or* blue?' Then swap places so that the child is asking you or another child whether you want X or Y.

9 **TEACHING TARGET: to use *or* in a sentence**

▶ **Games**

Race Board (Activity Sheet 1, Resources, p233), approximately 12 food pictures, counters, a die

Give the child learning the target the food pictures in two piles, face down. He will be the caller. When a player lands on a star, the caller turns over the top two cards and asks, for example, 'Do you like apple *or* pizza?' Continue in this way until someone reaches the end. Landing on a happy or sad face means moving forward or back one space.

10 **TEACHING TARGET: to use *if* in a sentence**

▶ **Hall/PE**

None

A game for a small group. The child learning the target will be the caller. Model the activity first by giving very simple instructions using *if*. For example, 'Sit down *if* I wave. Stand up *if* I clap.' Then let the child have a turn, helping him by saying the sentence together if necessary.

⑪ TEACHING TARGET: to use *if* in a sentence

▶ **Games**

A collection of animal and food pictures

A game for a small group. Shuffle the cards and deal one to each child in the group. The child learning the target is the caller. Model the sentence first, by saying 'Clap your hands *if* you have some food. Stand up *if* you have an animal.' Then let the child have a go, helping him out as above. When everyone has clapped or stood up, deal out another round of cards, and so on.

⑫ TEACHING TARGET: to use *if* in a sentence

▶ **Pencil & paper – Colouring Grid Game**

Photocopy of the grid sheet for each child (Activity Sheet 12, Resources, p253), colouring pencils, food pictures

Give each child a grid sheet. Give the child learning the target the food pictures in a pile face down. Model the sentence by taking the top picture and saying '*If* you like [eg] bananas, colour a square.' Repeat with another picture, then let the child have a go, helping him if necessary.

⑬ TEACHING TARGET: to use *when* in a sentence

▶ **Music**

Three or four different musicmakers

This is a version of the party game Musical Bumps. Model the sentence by saying, 'Sit down *when* I bang the drum.' The children then have to move around until you bang the drum. The last to sit down is out. Now let the child learning the target take over giving the instructions. Repeat with the other instruments.

⑭ TEACHING TARGET: to use *when* in a sentence

▶ **Hall/PE**

A ball

Model the target sentence as follows: 'Clap your hands *when* I throw the ball. Sit down *when* I bounce the ball. Hop *when* I roll the ball.' Then let the child learning the target give the instructions. Help as necessary.

⓯ **TEACHING TARGET: to use *when* in a sentence**

▶ **Hall/PE**

 Beanbags, pictures of food

Arrange the beanbags in a line at one end of the hall. Place the food pictures in a pile on the floor in front of you. Line up the children at the other end of the hall and explain that they are going to have a race. Model the sentence by taking the top food picture and saying 'Run to the beanbags *when* I say [eg] strawberries.' The children run to fetch a beanbag and bring it back. Replace the beanbags and repeat. Then let the child learning the target take over.

PART III ACTIVITIES FOR DEVELOPING SPEECH SOUNDS

CHECKLIST FOR PART III: DEVELOPING SPEECH SOUNDS

P Scale 5/6 Stage One 2–3 years equivalent	P Scale 6/7 Stage Two 3–4 years equivalent	P Scale 7/8 Stage Three 4–4.5 years equivalent	NC Level 1+ Stage Four 4.5–5 years equivalent
Does not use sounds *m, n, p, b, t, d*	Does not use sounds *c, g, f, s*	Does not use sounds *sh, ch, j, v z*	Does not use sound clusters (eg *sp, st, sk, pl, bl, cl, gl, fl*)

INTRODUCTION

There is an enormous variation in the speed at which young children learn to use the full range of speech sounds. Many of the pronunciation errors you may hear are part of a normal developmental process which involves the child simplifying the more complicated sounds. Incorrect vowel sounds are much rarer and require the help of a speech & language therapist. Table 1 shows typical immature consonant errors. A child needs help with speech sounds if:

- speech is very difficult to understand
- immaturities persist beyond the ages shown in Table 2
- the difficulties interfere with learning phonics.

Use the checklist on page 198 to work out which sounds you need to target.

TABLE 1

Problem	What child does	What it sounds like
back sounds *c/k, g*	bring them forward	*car = tar, game = dame*
friction sounds *f, s, sh, ch, j*	'stop' friction	*sea = tea, fish = pish*
r is too hard	use *w* instead	*red = wed*
clusters of consonants *sp, spr, fl*	leave some out	*spoon = poon, flower = fower*
consonants at end of word	leave them out	*bus = bu, dog = do*
unstressed syllables	leave them out	*banana = nana giraffe = raffe*
similar type sounds, eg *y/l*	use same sound twice	*yellow = lellow*

Table 2 overleaf shows a typical pattern of speech sound development.

TABLE 2 – NORMAL STEPS IN DEVELOPMENT OF SPEECH SOUNDS

Approximate chronological age	Consonants used	Description of speech
1 year–18 months		Any attempt at a word is acceptable. Pronunciation very inexact. May 'double' syllable (eg *bibit* for biscuit).
18 months–2 years	*m, n, p, b, t, d, w* Use of *h* emerging	May miss off final consonants (eg *bu* for bus).
2–2½ years	As above + *c*/*k* and *g* emerging	May still miss off final consonant. May make short sounds in place of longer ones, eg, *tea* for sea, *pish* for fish. May use a sound made at the front of the mouth in place of a back one, eg *tar* for car, *dirl* for girl. May not mark the difference between sounds using voice and 'whispered' sounds (*p*/*b*, *t*/*d*, *k*/*g*) so says, eg *goat* for both goat and coat.
2½–3 years	As above + *y, fl, sl, l* emerging	Speech understandable even by strangers. Consonant clusters often reduced to one component, eg *pane* for plane, *pot* for spot. May use substitutions for the more difficult groups of sound such as *sh*, *ch* and *j* so may say *fis* for fish, *dump* for jump.
3 years–4 years	As above, including *l*. Many consonant clusters now being used (eg *pl*, *br*, *sp*). *Sh*, *ch*, *j* emerging	May still be substituting short sounds for harder long ones eg *tair* for chair, *doo* for zoo. May still be reducing some consonant clusters. May use *w* or *y* for *l* (eg *wook* for look, *yeg* for leg).
4–4½ years	As above + *sh, ch, j, v, z* emerging. Most consonant clusters established	May still be muddling *w*, *y* and *l*. Some consonant clusters still reduced to one component
4½–5 years	Sound system nearly complete. *th* and *r* emerging	May be using *f* for *th* (eg *fink* for think. May use *w* for *r* (eg *wed* for red). These errors may persist until 6 years or later and are very usual. The use of *f* for *th* may be dialectal, ie it is the family speech pattern.

GENERAL ADVICE

1 The aim of this section is to teach the child to make new speech sounds at the beginning of single words and in two- or three-word phrases. The sounds chosen are those that most often cause difficulty.

2 It is very important to make clear, single sounds. This particularly applies to *p, t, c, k, f, s, sh, ch*. These are called 'voiceless' sounds because no voice is used. Therefore you can only say the whispered *p* without adding an 'uh' sound. *s, f, sh* become continuous sounds (ssss, ffff, shhh).

3 Speech difficulties that seem severe or include unusual sounds or sound substitutions should only be tackled under the guidance of a speech & language therapist.

4 Do not work on speech sounds until the child's language skills are reasonably established.

5 Do not work on speech sounds until the child's listening skills are secure.

6 If you do not have rapid success with helping the child make a new sound, do not persist. Try again another day. If you continue to have no success consider contacting a speech & language therapist.

7 Remember that it is quite easy for the child to learn to make a new sound. However, it is very difficult to establish the sound in everyday speech.

8 In general you should only work on one sound at a time, ignoring any other speech sound errors.

LEARNING STEPS

Learning new sounds involves the following stages:

1 Spotting the sound.

2 Making the sound.

3 Using the sound in nonsense words.

4 Using the sound in real words.

5 Using the sound in two word phrases.

6 Using the sound in short sentences.

WHERE TO START

1 Identify the sounds the child is not using (using the checklist).

2 Check these against the table of normal development (Table 2).

3 Go to the Learning Steps section (above) and work through it in order for each target sound.

Some children will move more quickly through these steps than others. However, it is vital that the child can hear the sound and discriminate between it and similar sounds before attempting to make the sound. The word lists included are for practice and have been chosen because the words are familiar and easy to draw There is a wide collection of activities at each step to choose from, according to the child's age and level of development.

DISCRIMINATION ACTIVITIES

ACTIVITY AREAS

- ▶ Construction & craft
- ▶ Home corner
- ▶ Hall/PE
- ▶ Circle games
- ▶ Games
- ▶ Tabletop games
- ▶ Storybooks

Before starting the MAKING SOUNDS section (p206) please refer to General Advice (2) on p201.

TEACHING IDEAS

① **TEACHING TARGET: to respond with an action to the target sound**

▶ **Construction & craft**

 Large bricks

Show the children that they are to make a big tower. Every time you make the 'special' sound they must put a brick on. They must wait and listen carefully each time. Make the target sounds for him, varying the time between signals from one to two or three seconds. Make sure he is waiting and responding to your signal.

② **TEACHING TARGET: to respond with an action to the target sound**

▶ **Home Corner**

 A large teddy or doll, toy food, a puppet

Give the child a collection of toy food items. Tell him that every time the puppet makes the target sound he must give a bit of food to the teddy or doll. Now make the sounds for him, varying the time between signals from a second to two or three seconds.

③ **TEACHING TARGET: to respond selectively to the target sound**

▶ **Hall/PE**

 Large hoops, CD/cassette player

Remind the children of the target sound. The children have to move around while the music is playing. When it stops, you will make the target sound or an animal noise. If they hear the target speech sound, they must go and sit in a hoop. If they hear an animal sound, they must stand still. This activity may prove too difficult. Try it two or three times on different occasions, but if the children still can't manage it, abandon it.

4 **TEACHING TARGET: to respond selectively to the target sound**

▶ **Circle games**

 A ball

Only try this game if the children were successful at the previous activity. Tell the children they are going to pass the ball round the circle. They must only pass it on if they hear the target sound. Now make a series of speech sounds, with the target sound included every so often. Correct at once if a child passes the ball on incorrectly, or fails to pass it on when he should. When it has gone right round the circle, let the children give themselves a clap.

5 **TEACHING TARGET: to be able to identify the target sound**

▶ **Sound pictures game**

 Pictures to represent the target sound and two other sounds

Teach the child to link speech sounds to pictures and the written letter. Any familiar picture can be used, or schemes such as Jolly Phonics if this is used in your school. Start with three sounds and three pictures. Show the child the pictures one at a time, saying the sound clearly at the same time. It is important to only say the actual sound, do not add a little 'uh' sound. The letter 's' is pronounced 'sssss', not 's-uh'. Lay the pictures out in front of the child. Say one of the sounds and see if he can point to the right picture. If not, go back to turning over each picture and telling him.

▶ **Lotto**

 Lotto board showing the pictures that represent the target sounds, small bricks or counters

The child will need to be familiar with at least four target sounds in order to play a Lotto game. Make a list of the sounds you are going to use. This should include the four the child knows and four unknown sounds. Play Lotto by calling a sound. If the child has that picture on his board he puts a counter or brick on the picture.

6 **TEACHING TARGET: to recognise the target sound**

▶ **Games**

 None

Introduce the sound to the child. Make it, show him how you are making it and do it a few times. Now tell him you are going to make a whole lot of speech sounds. When he hears the special target sound he is to say 'Stop.' Repeat several times. How often did he spot the target sound?

7 TEACHING TARGET: to recognise the target sound

▶ **Tabletop games**

Rubber mice, plastic cup, and computer mousepad

Give each child a mouse. The children place their mice on the mousepad, holding them tightly by the end of their tails. Say you are going to make lots of speech sounds. When they hear the target sound they must pull their mouse quickly out of the way, as that is when you are going to try to catch them by bringing the plastic cup down on top of them. Repeat the game several times, varying the order in which you say the sounds. How many times do they manage to escape?

8 TEACHING TARGET: to recognise the target sound at the beginning of a word

▶ **Games**

Small collection of objects and/or pictures, some of which begin with the target sound and some don't, a soft bag. To begin with, choose contrasting sounds widely different from the target sound (eg if target sound is *sh*: shoe, ship, shell, shop, shed, choose contrasting sounds *m*, *b*, *d*: mouse, man, bear, ball, dog, duck).

The children take turns to pull an object or picture out of the bag. You name the item, emphasising the target sound at first. The children have to say 'Yes' if it starts with the target sound, and 'No' if it doesn't. How many times can they get it right?

9 TEACHING TARGET: to recognise words starting with the target sound in a story

▶ **Storybooks**

A story which involves lots of words starting with the target sound, 'stop' sign

Tell the child you are going to read a story. Some of the words in the story begin with their current target sound. When they hear one of these words, they must hold up the 'Stop' sign. If you are playing with a group, they can all have something to use as a stop sign, or take turns to be the one holding the sign and giving you the signal to stop.

▶ **Circle games**

None

This is a game for a group of at least four children. Select two sounds the children are familiar with. Tell half the group to remember one of the sounds and the other half to remember the other sound. Sit them alternately according to which sound they are listening for. When they hear 'their' sound they must stand up. If it is not their sound they must sit down.

⓾ TEACHING TARGET: to be able to recognise the target sound

▶ **Home Corner**

 Large soft toy, toy food and a puppet

Give the child a collection of toy food items. Tell him that every time the puppet makes the target sound he must give a food item to the soft toy. Let him hear the puppet making the sound several times before you start. Then make a range of other single sounds, including the target sound, one at a time. Allow a few seconds for the child to think about the sound each time.

▶ **Listening game**

 None

In this game the children have to listen to you making sounds one at a time. Introduce the target sound, and make it a few times. Then tell them to listen carefully and if they hear that sound they must sit down as quickly as they can.

▶ **Hall/PE**

 Large hoops, music player

Introduce the target sound and say it several times. The children then have to move around while the music is playing. When it stops you will make a single speech sound. If it is the target sound, they must go and sit in a hoop. If it is not, they must stand still.

▶ **Tabletop games**

 Ten pictures of familiar objects, a box with the target sound written clearly on the side

Several (but not all) of the pictures should start with the target sound. Lay the pictures out face up on the table. Remind the child of the target sound again. Tell him you are going to try to find some pictures that start with that sound. Start by demonstrating yourself by picking up a picture, naming it, saying what the beginning sound is and then saying whether it can go in the target box or not. Now let the child have a go, helping him as soon as he seems unsure.

▶ **Snap game**

 A deck of picture cards, at least half of which start with the target sound

Shuffle the cards and deal. Remind the child of the target sound and explain that if two pictures start with that sound then it is Snap. You will need to demonstrate this first as it is not quite like the traditional game.

MAKING SOUNDS

SINGLE CONSONANTS – *p, b, m, t, d, c/k, g, f, s, sh, ch*

TEACHING IDEAS

MAKING THE SOUNDS *p, b*

Show the child how to put his lips together and 'blow' the sound out. Use a mirror so that he can copy what you are doing. Lots of children find it difficult to make a difference between *p* and *b*. Remember that *p* does not have an 'uh' added to it. Cut a little balloon shape out of tissue or thin paper. Stick it to the end of your finger. Show the child that when you say *p* the balloon moves. When you say *b* it does not.

Word list

pie

paw

pea

pen

bee

boy

bed

MAKING THE SOUND *m*

This is quite an easy sound to demonstrate, using a mirror as above. You can use cars or other vehicles to represent the *m* sound. Remember that it is a continuous sound (*mmm...*).

Word list

me

mum

man

more

MAKING THE SOUNDS *t, d*

These sounds are made by putting the tip of the tongue just behind the top front teeth and doing a little tapping movement. Remember not to add 'uh' when you say the sound *t*. You can help the child remember the sound by calling it eg 'the dripping tap sound' (*t*) or 'the drill sound' (*d*).

Word list

tea

toe

toy

two

door

door

dawn

dark

MAKING THE SOUND c

The most common sound substitution is using the *t* sound for *c* and the *d* sound for *g*. Both *c* and *g* are made by putting the back part of the tongue against the back of the roof of the mouth. The letters *c* and *k* make exactly the same sound. It is hard for a child to simply copy this because he cannot see what is happening when you make the sound. One way of helping, which often works, is to get the child to put his hand gently on the front of his neck as he tries to copy the sound. The feeling of the hand against the throat seems to stimulate the back of the tongue to move to the right position. Demonstrate what you want the child to do, then encourage him to have a go. If it does not work, don't worry, leave it and try again another time. If it does work, give him lots of praise, for example, 'Well done, you are so clever, you did the *c* sound just like me.' Then see if he can do it up to five times in a row. Each time he gets it right, put a brick on a tower or a counter in a pot, so he can see how well he is doing.

Word list

cow

key

case

car

card

cake

comb

MAKING THE SOUND g

The sound *g* is made in exactly the same way as *c/k*. Follow the instructions as above. The only difference is that the voice is *not* used with *c/k* and *is* used with *g*. Try it yourself. Make a *c* sound with your fingers lightly resting on your larynx (the 'voice box' at the front of your neck). You should not feel any kind of vibration. Now make a continuous humming sound. Your fingers should feel a vibration. Make the *g* sound and you should feel the vibration.

Word list

go

game

give

get

ghost

goal

MAKING THE SOUND *f*

Use a mirror that is big enough for you and the child to see each other. Explain that you must gently bite your top teeth on your bottom lip and blow. Demonstrate doing this to the child. Then encourage him to have a go at the same time as you, looking in the mirror to compare. If he finds it very difficult after a few tries, leave it and try again another day. If he succeeds give him lots of praise.

Word list

four

fish

foot

feet

face

farm

fan

MAKING THE SOUND *s*

Explain to the child that *s* is a hissy sound, like a snake. Show him by making a long *sssssssssss*. Then tell him how to do it himself. He needs to bite his back teeth together gently and push the hissy noise through his teeth. Encourage him to have a go. If the sound seems to be coming from the sides of his mouth and does not sound quite right, leave it and try again another time. If it sounds more like *th* remind him to put his back teeth together. Give him lots of praise if he succeeds.

Word list

sea

sun

sand

sock

soup

soap

seat

Making the sound *sh* as in *shoe*

This is a whispered sound. Make sure you only say the *sh* part, as in telling a child to keep quiet ('shhhhh'). Tell the child to bite his back teeth together, make his lips round and blow. Do it yourself so that he can see the lip shape. Use a mirror if it helps.

Word list

shoe

shed

shell

ship

shop

sheep

shade

shore

shape

Making the sound *ch* as in *chop*

Do not try this sound until the child can do *sh*. This is a whispered sound. Make sure you only say the *ch* sound as in the old-fashioned train noise. Tell the child to bite his back teeth together, make his lips round and *push* the sound out. If the child recognises the letter 't', write it on a piece of paper and tell him to make the 't' sound first.

Word list
chair
chin
cheek
chain
chip
cheese
chopper

CONSONANT CLUSTERS – *pl, bl, cl, gl, fl, sp, st, sc/k, sl, sm, sn, sw*

The sounds in this section all involve pairs of consonants. These will be referred to as *consonant clusters. It is very important that the child can pronounce both consonants singly before you attempt this section.* For example, before working on the sound cluster *pl*, make sure the child can say words that start with *p* and words that start with *l* before you start.

How to teach clusters

The procedure for learning to make the sounds is the same for all the consonant clusters. Explain to the child that he is going to learn to say two sounds together. Write each sound in large clear print on separate sheets of paper. Place them on the table or floor, leaving a big gap between them. Make the sounds one at a time, pointing to the letters at the same time. Gradually move the sheets closer together and make the sounds as close together as possible. Encourage the child to copy you. If he is successful you can start to work through the speech activities.

CONSONANT CLUSTERS WORD LISTS

pl word list
plate
plane
plug
plant
planet
plaster
plait

bl word list
blue
black
blade
blow

cl word list
clock
clap
clay
class
clip

gl word list
glue
glass

fl word list
fly
flag
flower
flame
flip-flop

sm word list
smile
smell
small
smoothie

sp word list
spoon
spider
spot
spade
space

st word list
step
stair
stop
stick
stool

sc/k word list
school
sky
skirt
scarf
skin

sn word list
snow
snail
snip
snap

sl word list
slug
slide
sleep
slow

sw word list
swing
sweets
swim

PRACTISING SOUNDS

TEACHING IDEAS

1 **TEACHING TARGET: to make the target sound**

▶ **Games**

A mirror, a puppet (doll or animal) whose mouth opens

The child should now be familiar with the sound you are working on. Tell him that the time has come to learn how to make it himself. He may already have done so spontaneously during the previous activities. Depending on your knowledge of the child, you may decide to teach him in a one-to-one situation or in a small group of children at a similar stage. Show him how to make the sound. Use the mirror or the puppet as extra aids if necessary.

Hold up five fingers. Ask the child to 'knock down' one finger at a time by making the special sound. See if he can do it five times so that all your fingers are closed into a fist.

▶ **Hall/PE**

A beanbag

The children stand around you in a circle. Throw the beanbag to a child, making the target sound as you do so. He must throw it back to you, making the sound at the same time. Continue round the circle in this way.

▶ **Hall/PE**

Skipping ropes and balls

The adult and child each hold an end of a skipping rope. Swing the rope gently back and forward, saying the target sound as the rope swings. Repeat about six times. Then sit opposite each other in pairs. Roll the ball from one to the other, each person making the sound as he rolls it. Again repeat about six times.

▶ **Hall/PE**

A chalked out large ladder on the floor

Show the children how to walk along the ladder step by step, saying the target sound as they step on each rung.

▶ **Circle games**

None

This game is for when the children have learnt to recognise and make several of the Stage One sounds. The children are to be parrots and copy the sounds you make. Have something to hold up in front of your face to hide your mouth. Choose a child, hide your face, and make one of the target sounds. Can he copy you? Repeat with another child and a different sound, and so on round the circle.

▶ **Counters game**

Counters

Show the child how to make the sound. Can he do it? Hurrah. Challenge him to a little competition. Start off with ten counters between you. Every time he gets the sound right, he gets a counter. When he says it wrong, you get a counter. See if he can win five counters.

▶ **Hall**

Two skipping ropes, chalk. Lay out the ropes parallel to each other, with two or three metres between them. Place the 'stepping stones' in a wiggly line between the ropes, to represent stepping stones across a river.

Tell the children they have to get across the river, stepping on one stone at a time, and saying the target sound at each step. If this proves easy, speed up the crossing by telling the children a crocodile is approaching.

▶ **Circle games**

A beanbag

Tell the children they are going to pass the beanbag round the circle. As they pass it to their next-door neighbour they must say the target sound. They are to keep it going as quickly as possible. When you say 'All change' they must start it going round the other way. Repeat several times.

❷ TEACHING TARGET: to be able to use the sound in a nonsense word

▶ **Pencil & paper**

Four 'monsters' drawn on separate sheets of paper

Give each monster a name. This will be a short nonsense word, consisting of the target sound and a vowel sound. It does not matter whether the target sound is at the beginning or the end – whichever the child finds easiest to say accurately. For example, target sound 's' – *Sar, Sor, Say* or *Ees, Oos, Ors*. Practise saying the monsters' names together at first. If there is one that the child finds particularly difficult, leave that one out for the time being. Once he can copy you saying the name you can give the child opportunities to say it on his own. Get him to hide his eyes, remove a monster and see if he can tell you which one is missing. Spread out the pictures on the floor. The child has to tell you which monster to jump on. You can introduce variety by having balloons, witches or racing cars instead of monsters. The principle is the same: practising the new sound in a nonsense word.

▶ **Tabletop games**

The Race Board (Activity Sheet 1, Resources, p233). List of nonsense words consisting of the target sound + long vowel. In some the vowel comes before the target sound, and in others it comes after. (Example: *sh – shoo, shee, shay, shar, shoh, shor, shie, show, oosh, eesh, aysh, arsh, ohsh, orsh, owsh*.) Obviously some of these sound like real words, but present them as nonsense

An activity for two or more children. Play the game as a normal race game, but whenever a child lands on a star he has to say one of the nonsense words. Say the words for the children to copy, emphasising the target sound. Try them with the target sound in both initial and final positions in the nonsense words. Some children find one easier than the other. If one sound position proves particularly hard for a child, abandon it for the time being and concentrate on the other. Come back to the hard one later.

❸ TEACHING TARGET: to be able to use the target sound in a single word

▶ **Pairs game**

Two identical sets of pictures of familiar items that either start or end with the target sound

Play the Pairs game (Resources, p219). Put all the cards face down on the table and take turns to pick up two cards. The child must say the names of both pictures and keep them if they are a pair.

▶ Race game

Race Board (Activity Sheet 1, Resources, p233), copied onto card, a die, counters, set of pictures containing the target sound

If the child lands on a star he takes a card from the pile. If he says it correctly he moves forward a space. If incorrect he moves back a space. The happy/sad faces also mean moving forward or back.

▶ Kim's Game

A set of small objects starting with the target sound

Put the objects on a tray and name them all with the child. Let him have a chance to look and memorise where they are. He then turns away while you remove an object. He has to try to tell you what is missing.

▶ Fishing game

Pictures containing target word with paper clips attached, 'fishing rod' (eg a chopstick with a small magnet attached on a string)

Lay the pictures face down on the floor. Take turns to 'fish' for one. The child must say the name of the picture. If he says it right he keeps the 'fish'.

④ TEACHING TARGET: to use the target sound at the beginning of short easy words

▶ Tabletop games

Snakes and Ladders game, list of words using the target sound

Play Snakes and Ladders in the usual way. When you come to a ladder you are only allowed to go up it if you say one of the words on the list correctly. You tell the child what word he is to say each time.

▶ Tabletop games

Pictures of objects or actions starting with the target sound, the Race Board game (Activity Sheet 1, Resources, p233), counters

Place the pile of pictures face down on the table. Play the race board game in the usual way. When anybody lands on a penalty square, they must turn over a card and name the picture. Other players can challenge if they think the word is not pronounced correctly. It is a good idea for the adult to make the occasional deliberate error. A counter is awarded for every correct word.

⑤ TEACHING TARGET: to be able to use the target sound in a two-word phrase

▶ **Pairs game**

Line drawings of objects starting with the target sound

You will need two pictures of each object. Colour one red and the other blue. Put the pictures face down and play the Pairs game in the usual way. The child must say both words (eg 'red car') when he turns over the picture. If the objects match he keeps the pair.

▶ **Race game**

Race Board (Activity Sheet 1, Resources, p233), pictures of target words, die, counters

You need to have a big and a little version of each target word. Play the Race Board game in the usual way. When the child lands on a star he takes a picture from the pile and tells you what it is (eg 'a little car'). If he says the target word correctly, he moves forward a space. Use the happy/sad faces to move forward and back as well.

▶ **Shopping game**

Objects starting with the target sound, at least two of each

Get the child to name all the objects before you start. If he gets the target sound right, carry on with the game. He goes to the 'shop' and brings you two objects. They may be the same or different. He tells you what he has brought, for example, 'one car, one coat' or 'two keys'. This gives practice saying the word in a short phrase.

▶ **Tabletop games**

Rough line drawings on cards showing the target sounds in as many words as possible

Let the children colour in the pictures. Each child chooses a different colour and colours three or four pictures. Mix up all the pictures and give each child a hand of cards. In turn, each child turns over one of his cards and holds it up. Everybody else must have a go at saying what it is (eg for *sh*: a blue shoe, a red ship, a black sheep). Even if the child has been naming single words beautifully, this step often proves really hard. Help the child go slowly if necessary at first, saying 'blue – shoe, red – ship', until it gets easier.

6 **TEACHING TARGET: to be able to use the target sound in a short sentence**

▶ **Hiding game**

Two sets of pictures containing the target sound

The child takes four pictures from his pack and puts them in a line, face up on the table. You choose one of the same pictures from your pack but do not let him see it. He has to ask the question 'Is it a …?' until he gets the right picture, which he then keeps. Continue with another four cards.

▶ **Stepping Stones game**

Pictures of the target words

Attach the pictures to larger sheets of paper, which will be 'stepping stones'. The child then tells you or others in the group to 'Jump on the …' or 'Step over the …'

▶ **Pencil & paper**

Pictures of the words involving target sounds, paper and pencil, some bricks

The child has the pictures, concealed from you. He looks at the top picture and gives you the instruction 'Draw a …'. If he says the target word correctly he starts a tower with the bricks. He then continues to tell you what to draw, adding bricks to his tower if he says the target word right. When the child has reached this step the sound is beginning to be established. He will still make mistakes in his everyday speech but this is part of the normal learning process.

PART IV RESOURCES

GAMES & RHYMES

THERAPY GAMES

BARRIER GAME

A matching game for an adult and one child. The two participants sit opposite each other, with a screen between them so that they cannot see what the other person is doing. Players have identical sets of objects or pictures, in a box. The adult puts one or more of her objects or pictures on the table in front of her. She tells the child what he needs to do to match her arrangement. Time is allowed for the child to comply. Lift the screen, and hey presto! Is he right? The objects or pictures are replaced in the box and a new arrangement set out.

This game can be used both as a teaching tool and for checking understanding. It can also be used as an expressive language activity, letting the child take the role of the 'instructor'.

If you are putting out two or more pictures or objects in a row, remember to arrange yours from *right to left*, so that they will correspond with the child's arrangement. He should be putting his out from *left to right*.

Examples

- Each player has set of animals. Easy: 'Put out a giraffe' (replace it in the box). 'Find an elephant', and so on. Harder: 'Find a giraffe and an elephant.' Harder still: 'Put out a camel, a cow and a horse.'
- Each player has a set of action pictures: 'Find somebody crying.' 'Find somebody laughing.'
- Each player has a set of coloured pictures: 'Find the blue hat.' 'Find a green coat.'
- Each player has a set of miniature animals, a house, and a tree: 'Put a dog behind the house.' 'Put a cat beside the tree.'

FEELY BAG GAME

Single objects or several objects are put into a soft bag. Children may be invited to feel one object and guess what it is, or to identify one object from the rest by feel. This game can also be used to practise describing words (the child is asked to say what an object feels like – soft, squashy, hard, square, round).

PAIRS

The Pairs game needs two identical sets of pictures. The pairs are laid out on the table in random order, to form a square or rectangle. For very young immature children, the game should be introduced with not more than about six pairs, laid out in four rows of three or three rows of four. The number can be increased as appropriate. The two players alternate in turning up a pair of cards, looking for a matching pair. If the pair doesn't match, the pictures are replaced face down in their original position. When a matching pair is turned up, the player keeps the pair. The winner is the one with the most cards at the end. The important thing when playing this game as a speech & language technique is that the child names each picture as he turns it over.

RACE BOARD GAME (see Activity Sheet 1, Resources, p233)

The Race Board is a standard Start to Finish game using a die and a counter or token for each child. Most of the games involve a specific deck of cards which give the child a task. When a player lands on a star square they take a card from the deck. If a player lands on a happy face they move forward one space. If they land on a sad face they move back one space.

SHOPPING GAME

An assortment of objects is set out on a table. The child is given a bag, and asked to go to the 'shop', 'buy' an item, put it in his bag and bring it to the adult. This activity can be extended until the child is being asked to fetch two, three or four items at a time. The objects are replaced in the shop between turns. It can be made into more of a game by having another child act as 'shopkeeper'. Ask the child what he has got in his bag when he brings it to you. Can he remember?

COMMERCIAL GAMES

MOUSIE-MOUSIE

This is a commercial game but you could make one quite easily. You need a 'mouse' with a long tail for each player, a round base to put the mouse on and a plastic cup. The players put their mice on the base and hold the tails. Explain that you will make some sounds and when they hear the target sound they must quickly pull away their mouse before you catch it with the cup.

PICTURE DOMINOES

The dominoes are shared out among the players. One player puts down a domino. The next player tried to find a domino with a picture that matches either end of the first one. He places his domino with the two matching pictures next to each other. The other players take turns to find a domino that can continue this line. Anyone who cannot do so misses a turn. The winner is the first to get rid of all his dominoes. The child is encourage to name his picture as he places his domino.

PICTURE LOTTO

Each player has a different board with about six to eight pictures on it. One player is chosen to be the caller and has a deck of all of the pictures face down on the table. He says each picture name as he turns it over. If it matches a player's board they shout 'Mine!' and place that picture on their board. The first player to cover all their pictures is the winner.

SNAKES AND LADDERS

Each player needs a counter or token. The first player rolls the die and moves forward that number of spaces. If a player lands on a ladder they move to the space at the top of it. If they land on a snake they move to the space at the bottom of it. The first to reach the end is the winner.

SNAP

The cards are divided equally among the players and put face down. The players take turns to turn over a card and put it on one of two central piles. If two identical cards appear on the central piles the first player to shout 'Snap!' takes the piles. Any player who loses all his cards is out and the winner is either the player to win all the cards, or the player with the most cards when time runs out.

PARTY AND TRADITIONAL GAMES

THE FARMER'S IN THE DELL

This is a game for a group. Choose a child to be the farmer. The rest of the group form a circle around the farmer. They hold hands and move round singing:

> The farmer's in his dell,
> The farmer's in his dell,
> Ee Aye, Ee Aye,
> The farmer's in his dell.
> The farmer wants a wife,
> The farmer wants a wife,
> Ee Aye, Ee Aye,
> The farmer wants a wife.

The farmer then chooses a child to join him in the middle of the circle as his 'wife'. The children join hands again and sing: 'The wife wants a child' etc. 'The wife' then chooses a 'child'. The children join hands and sing: 'The child wants a dog' etc. and a 'dog' is chosen. The children join hands and sing: 'The dog wants a bone' etc. and a bone is chosen. The farmer, wife, child and dog then *gently* pat the 'bone' while those on the outside of the circle sing:

> We all pat the bone,
> We all pat the bone,
> Ee Aye, Ee Aye,
> We all pat the bone.

GRANDMOTHER'S FOOTSTEPS

A group game to be played in a large space, for example the hall or playground. Choose a child to be 'grandmother'. He stands facing the wall at one end of the space. The rest of the group line up side by side at the other end of the space facing Grandmother. They must slowly and quietly creep forward while Grandmother is facing the wall, but stop the second she turns round. Anyone still moving has to go back to the beginning and start again. If a child manages to reach Grandmother and tap her on the back before she turns round, he takes her place and the game starts again.

HERE WE GO ROUND THE MULBERRY BUSH

A game for a group of children. Everyone joins hands in a circle and moves round singing:

> Here we go round the mulberry bush,
> The mulberry bush, the mulberry bush,
> Here we go round the mulberry bush on a cold and frosty morning.

The adult then chooses an action to add to the song, for example:

> This is the way we wash our hands,
> Wash our hands, wash our hands,
> This is the way we wash our hands on a cold and frosty morning.

The children mime the action as they join in with the words. Repeat with other actions, eg 'brush our hair'.

HIDE AND SEEK

There are many different ways of playing Hide and Seek. In this version one child is chosen to be the 'hider'. When he has hidden, with help if necessary, the rest of the group go to find him.

HOPSCOTCH

A hopscotch grid is drawn on the playground with chalk. There are lots of versions of this traditional game. The simplest is for the child simply to hop from one side of the grid to the other without stepping on the lines.

HUNT THE THIMBLE

A hiding game. One child goes out of the room while you hide a small object. Call him back in to try to find it. The rest of the group can indicate whether he is getting nearer or further away by saying 'You're getting warmer, no, cooler now, a bit warmer, really hot,' etc.

KIM'S GAME

Version A

You need a collection of not more than 12 small objects, a tray and a cloth to cover them. Put all the objects on the tray and show each one to the child, naming it as you do so. Allow the child a short time to look at the objects, then cover them with the cloth. The child has to tell you as many of the objects as he can remember.

Version B

As above only this time you cover the objects and remove one without the child seeing. He has to try to tell you what is missing.

ORANGES AND LEMONS

Two children hold both hands high to form an arch. The rest of the group go under the arch, one behind the other, whilst singing the song. When they reach the last line of the song the two children forming the arch try to catch a child by bringing down their arms over his head.

> Oranges and lemons,
> Say the bells of St Clement's.
> You owe me five farthings,
> Say the bells of St Martin's.
>
> When will you pay me?
> Say the bells of Old Bailey.
> When I grow rich,
> Say the bells of Shoreditch.
> When will that be?
> Say the bells of Stepney.
> I do not know,
> Says the great bell of Bow.
>
> Here comes a candle
> To light you to bed,
> Here comes a chopper
> To chop off your head!
> Chop! Chop! CHOP! (Catching child who is under the arch.)

PASS THE PARCEL

You need a small 'prize' and a music player. Wrap up the prize and continue adding layers of wrapping paper until there are enough for everyone in the group to have a turn at unwrapping. Sit the children in a circle and give the parcel to one child. The children must pass the parcel round the circle while the music is playing. When it stops the child holding the parcel takes off one layer of wrapping. Continue in this way, keeping track of who has had a turn. Written 'forfeits' may be included between the wrappings, which can be read out for a child or the whole group to carry out.

PIN THE TAIL ON THE DONKEY

Draw an outline of a donkey without a tail on a large sheet of paper. Stick the picture on a wall. Make a tail out of plaited wool or a paper cut-out. Use a scarf as a blindfold. Show the children the drawing and explain that they have to try to put the tail in the right place with the blindfold on. Choose a confident child to start. Tie the blindfold loosely and gently turn the child round a couple of times, leaving him facing the picture of the donkey. Give him the tail and guide him to the wall with the picture on. He has to try to put the tail in the right place. Mark his choice by writing his initials on the picture. Repeat with all the children in the group. The child whose tail was nearest the correct position is the winner.

SIMON SAYS (see Activity Sheet 3, Resources, p237 for sample instructions)

One person is chosen to be the caller. The rest of the group stand well apart, facing the caller. The caller then gives instructions to the group. They must only respond to instructions that start with 'Simon says'. Anyone carrying out an instruction that does not start with 'Simon says' is out.

STATUES

Another musical game for a group of children. Explain to them that while the music is playing they must dance and move around. As soon as the music stops they must keep absolutely still whatever position they are in. Anyone moving after the music stops is out.

ADDITIONAL RHYMES

TWO LITTLE DICKY BIRDS

To accompany this rhyme you need to put a small piece of coloured sticky paper over the nail of each of your two forefingers. These are the 'dicky birds'. Make the rest of your fingers into fists so that just your two forefingers are displayed. As you say 'Two little dicky birds sitting on a wall' tap the table with your forefingers. As you say 'One named Peter' tap one finger on the table and tap the other finger as you say 'One named Paul.' On the line 'Fly away Peter' put the Peter hand over your shoulder or behind your back, tuck the forefinger in and bring your hand back showing only the middle finger. 'Peter' is no longer there. Repeat with the other hand, making 'Paul' disappear. When you get to the line 'Come back Peter', reverse the process, putting your hand out of sight, changing the fingers and bringing the forefinger with the coloured paper back into view. Repeat with 'Come back Paul'.

TWO LITTLE DICKY BIRDS

> Two little dicky birds, sitting on a wall,
> One named Peter, one named Paul.
> 'Fly away Peter, fly away Paul.'
> 'Come back Peter, come back Paul.'

FIVE LITTLE DUCKS

> Five little ducks went swimming one day
> Over the hills and far away.
> Mummy duck said 'Quack, quack, quack, quack!'
> But only four little ducks came back.

Four little ducks went swimming one day
Over the hills and far away.
Mummy duck said 'Quack, quack, quack, quack!'
But only three little ducks came back.

(continue in this way until no ducks come back)

FIVE LITTLE MONKEYS

Five little monkeys jumping on the bed.
One fell off and bumped his head.
Mummy phoned the doctor
And the doctor said,
That's what you get for jumping on the bed.

Repeat with four, three, two little monkeys, etc.

HEADS, SHOULDERS, KNEES AND TOES

Heads, shoulders, knees and toes,
Knees and toes,
Heads, shoulders, knees and toes,
Knees and toes,
And eyes and mouth and ears and nose,
Heads, shoulders, knees and toes,
Knees and toes.

THE HOKEY COKEY

You put your left arm in, your left arm out
In out, in out, you shake it all about
You do the Hokey Cokey and you turn around
That's what it's all about
Whoa-o the Hokey Cokey
Whoa-o the Hokey Cokey
Whoa-o the Hokey Cokey
Knees bent, arms stretched
Raa raa raa

(continue in this way, with *right arm*, *left leg*, *right leg*, *whole self*)

IF YOU'RE HAPPY AND YOU KNOW IT

If you're happy and you know it clap your hands.
If you're happy and you know it clap your hands.
If you're happy and you know it then you really want to show it.
If you're happy and you know it clap your hands.

Repeat with *stamp your feet, touch your nose, wave your hand* and so on.

I HEAR THUNDER

I hear thunder. I hear thunder.
Oh don't you? Oh don't you?
Pitter patter raindrops. Pitter patter raindrops.
I'm wet through. So are you.

INCY WINCY SPIDER

Incy Wincy spider climbed up the spout,
Down came the rain and washed the spider out.
Out came the sun and dried up all the rain.
Incy Wincy spider climbed up the spout again.

LITTLE BOY BLUE

Little boy blue
Come blow up your horn.
The sheep's in the meadow,
The cow's in the corn.
But where is the boy
Who looks after the sheep?
He's under a haystack,
Fast asleep!

OLD MACDONALD

Old Macdonald had a farm
Ee i ee i o
And on his farm he had some chicks
Ee i ee i o
With a cluck-cluck here
And a cluck-cluck there
Here a cluck, there a cluck
Everywhere a cluck-cluck
Old Macdonald had a farm
Ee i ee i o

Add in other animals as follows:
cows – moo-moo
dogs – woof-woof
cat – meow-meow
sheep – baa-baa
horses – neigh-neigh
pigs – oink-oink

ONE FINGER, ONE THUMB

One finger, one thumb keep moving, One finger, one thumb keep moving,
One finger, one thumb keep moving, we'll all be merry and bright.
One finger, one thumb, one arm keep moving, One finger, one thumb, one arm keep moving,
One finger, one thumb, one arm keep moving, we'll all be merry and bright.

Continue adding a leg, etc.

ONE LITTLE FINGER

One little finger, one little finger,
One little finger tap, tap, tap.
Point to the ceiling. Point to the floor.
And put it in your lap.

Repeat with two fingers, etc.

PANCAKE POEM

Mix a pancake, stir a pancake, pop it in the pan.
Fry the pancake, toss the pancake, catch it if you can.

(Christina Rossetti)

PUSSY CAT, PUSSY CAT

Pussy cat, pussy cat,
Where have you been?
'I've been up to London to look at the Queen.'
Pussy cat, pussy cat,
What did you there?
'I frightened a little mouse under her chair.'

RING A RING O' ROSES

Ring a ring o' roses
A pocket full of posies.
Attishoo, Attishoo!
We all fall down!

The cows are in the meadow
Eating buttercups.
Attishoo, Attishoo!
We all jump up!

ROW, ROW THE BOAT

Row, row, row the boat
Gently down the stream.
Merrily, merrily, merrily, merrily,
Life is but a dream.

TEN IN THE BED

There were ten in the bed and the little one said,
'Roll over, roll over!'
So they all rolled over and one fell out,
There were nine in the bed and the little one said,
'Roll over, roll over!'
So they all rolled over and one fell out,
There were eight in the bed and the little one said,
'Roll over, roll over!'

(and so on until there are none in the bed)

WHEELS ON THE BUS

The wheels on the bus go round and round, round and round. round and round.
The wheels on the bus go round and round,
all day long!

The people on the bus go up and down, up and down, up and down.
The people on the bus go up and down,
all day long!

The horn on the bus goes beep, beep, beep,beep, beep beep, beep, beep, beep.
The horn on the bus goes beep, beep, beep.
all day long!

The wipers on the bus go swish, swish, swish, swish, swish, swish. swish, swish, swish.
The wipers on the bus go swish, swish, swish,
all day long!

The engine on the bus goes zoom, zoom, zoom, zoom, zoom, zoom, zoom, zoom, zoom.
The engine on the bus goes zoom, zoom, zoom,
all day long!

The babies on the bus go waa, waa, waa, waa, waa, waa, waa, waa, waa.
The babies on the bus go waa, waa, waa,
all day long!

The parents on the bus go shh, shh, shh, shh, shh, shh, shh, shh, shh.
The parents on the bus go shh, shh, shh,
all day long!

TECHNIQUES

This section explains a range of techniques used by speech & language therapists to encourage understanding and use of language.

CLOZE PROCEDURE

Similar to the cloze procedure used in written work but here used in spoken activities. The adult leaves a gap in a familiar song, rhyme or story for the child to fill in. The procedure can be used to prompt a single word, short phrase, or longer sentence.

Examples

Row, row, row your boat, gently down the stream.
If you see a crocodile don't forget to … (scream).

Humpty Dumpty sat on the … (wall).
Humpty Dumpty sat on … (the wall).
Humpty Dumpty … (sat on the wall).

Then the big, bad wolf said 'I'll huff, and I'll puff, and …' (I'll blow your house down).

EXPANDING SENTENCES

Repetition of a child's attempt at a phrase or sentence, and adding another idea to it.

Example

Child: 'I got a bus.'
Adult: 'Yes, you've got the blue bus' or, at a more advanced level, 'Yes, you've got the bus with the driver in.' This confirms the child's attempt and models for him how he could enlarge on a sentence type that he can already manage.

FORCED ALTERNATIVES

Offering two modelled words, phrases or sentences for the child to choose between and copy in order to say what he wants.

Examples

'Do you want the *car* or the *train*?' ('Train').
'Do you want the *blue car* or the *red car*?' ('Red car').
'Do you want to *play in the sand* or *look at a book*?' ('Play in the sand.')

INFORMATION WORDS

Look at the following scenario. On the floor there is a car, a ball, a chair and a box. This is an example of what you might typically say to the child:

'What I want you to do is put the *car behind* the *chair*.'

This sentence has 13 words but only three of them are the words the child has to understand to carry out the instruction (*car, behind, chair*). These words are called information words.

At this level information words could be naming words, action words, describing words and position words.

Examples

Granny is *kicking* the *ball*	naming word, action word, naming word (person action object)
Kick the *ball* to *granny*	action word, naming word, naming word (action object person)
The *cup* is on *daddy's table*	naming word, naming word, naming word (object possession object)
The *hat* is *under* the *carpet*	naming word, position word, naming word (object preposition place)
Put the *book on* the *big* box	naming word, position word, describing word (object place adjective)
Give the *little ball* to *daddy*	describing word, naming word, naming word (adjective object person)

When setting up the activity you must make sure that each of the words in italics has a contrast. For example *Granny (mummy)* is *kicking (throwing)* the *ball (apple)*.

If the child has difficulty carrying out the command try reducing the number of information words. You do this by removing one of the contrasts. Using the above example, if you take away the apple, the sentence then contains two information words: *Granny (mummy)* is *kicking (throwing)* the ball.

Teaching activities are given for each sentence type at Stages Two, Three and Four. You can vary the equipment suggested to suit the needs of individual children. Children at Stage One would not necessarily be expected to understand sentences with three information words.

MODELLING

Supplying the word, phrase or sentence that the child would be likely to use himself if he were able to, and/or that you want to teach.

Example

'You're putting sand in your bucket. Now you're putting more in.'

PLAY (Parallel)

Play in which an adult involves herself in an activity of the child's choosing. It resembles the instinctive way in which a mother plays with a very young child. The adult plays alongside the child, following his lead, without any attempt to direct his actions. The adult maintains a commentary on what both participants are doing, supplying the language and vocabulary that the child himself lacks and including teaching targets.

Principles are:

- Follow the child's lead in play
- Keep language natural, and sentences short and simple
- Talk about what is happening here and now (immediacy)
- Avoid asking questions
- Use lots of repetition

Example

> Play activity with trains and a train track. Typical commentary: 'Here's my engine. My train's going this way. Through the tunnel. Oh, crash! Your train's going backwards, isn't he? Mine's going up the hill. Up the hill, up the hill. Oh dear, it's fallen off. I'll put it back on. On you go. Here comes your train. Whee! He's blowing his whistle.'

PLAY (Extended)

Play in which an adult involves herself in an activity which the child enjoys, follows his lead, but suggests new ideas to broaden and vary the play. This allows opportunities for the introduction of a greater range of language and vocabulary targets.

Example

> Play activity with the farm, farm animals and playmat. The child has concentrated for several minutes on lining all the animals up in a row. You want to teach some action words. Typical commentary: 'That's a lovely long line. Now shall we put them in the field? Here's a cow – shall we put it in there? Here's another cow for you – make it walk into the field. Here's another cow. And here comes a horse. Make him run into the field. I'll walk this horse in. Here comes the farmer. He wants to feed the animals.'

REINFORCEMENT

Repetition of a child's attempt at a word, phrase or sentence.

Example

> Child: 'I got bus.'
> Adult, 'Yes, you've got a bus.' This shows the child he has been understood, starts to build a conversation and also models the correct sentence form.

ROLE REVERSAL

This involves letting the child take the 'teacher' role. After carrying out a game or activity in which the adult takes the lead, give the child a chance to tell you or the other children what to do in the same activity.

ACTIVITY SHEETS

ACTIVITY SHEETS FOR UNDERSTANDING LANGUAGE PART I

Some activities are not used in Part I

ACTIVITY SHEETS FOR UNDERSTANDING LANGUAGE PART II

Some activities are not used in Part II

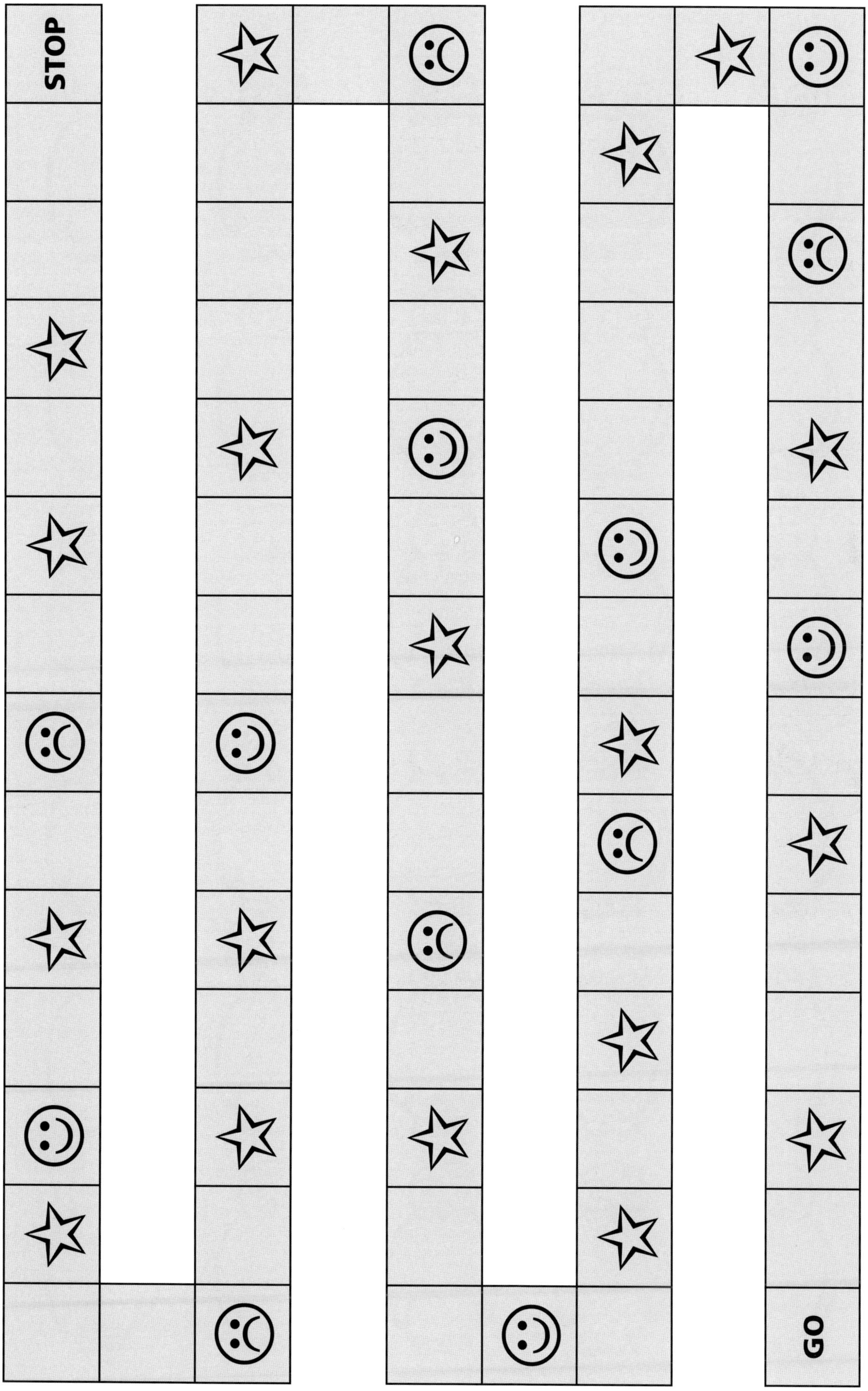
STOP
GO

Photocopy the sheet and cut squares out, then give each child an owl.

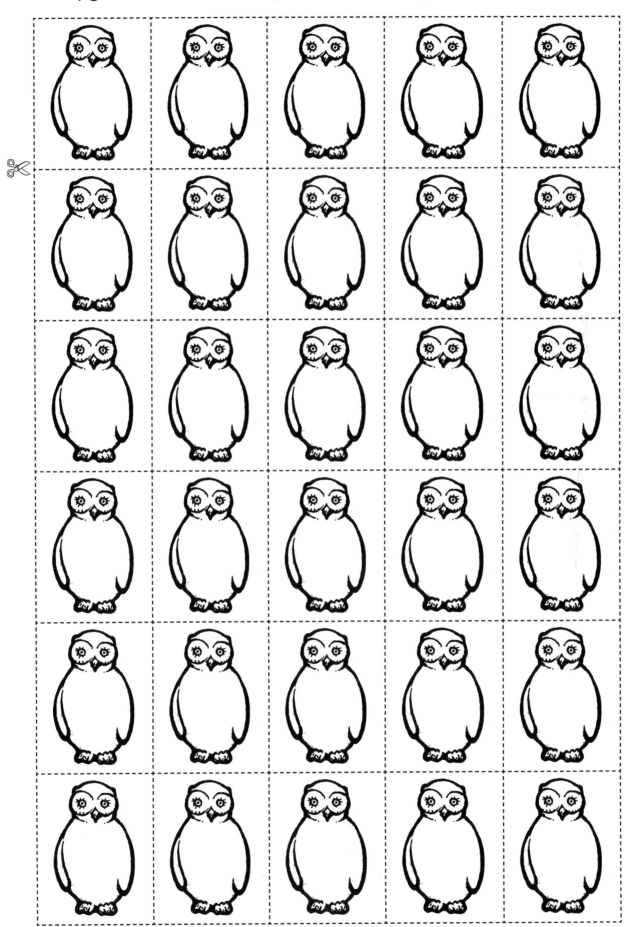

You can photocopy this sheet and enlarge it, so that there is enough room for all the children to put their owl on the tree.

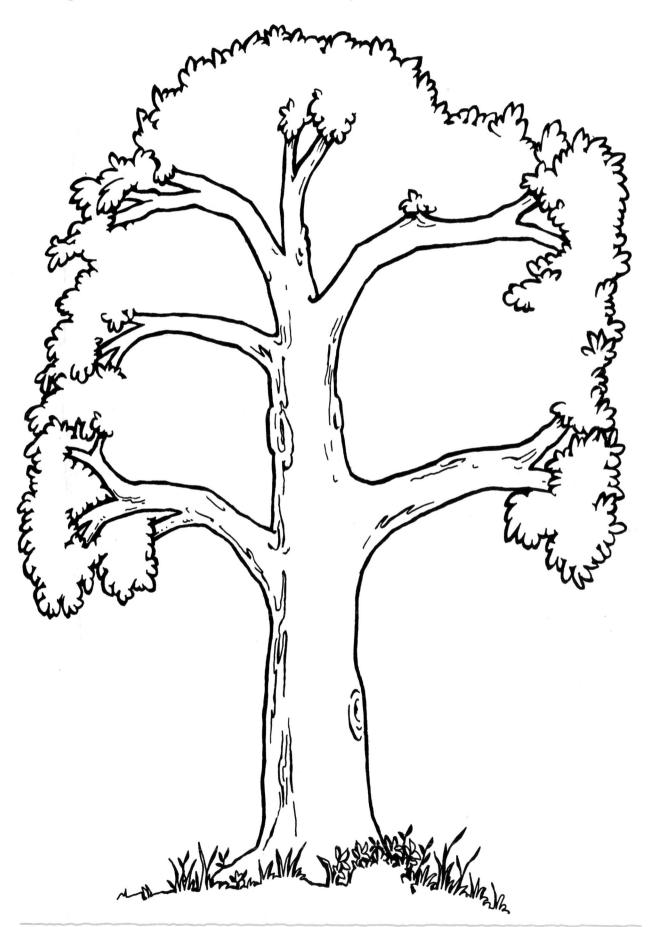

Go to a high branch	Go to a low branch
Go to a high branch	Go to a low branch
Go to a high branch	Go to a low branch
Go to a high branch	Go to a low branch
Go to a high branch	Go to a low branch
Go to a high branch	Go to a low branch

SIMON SAYS

1 Simon says, 'Stand on one foot and wave your hand.'

2 Simon says, 'Put your foot down and stop waving.'

3 Sit on the floor and shut your eyes.

4 Simon says, 'Turn around and sit on the floor.'

5 Clap your hands.

6 Simon says, 'Shut your eyes and point to the ceiling.'

7 Simon says, 'Open your eyes and stop pointing.'

8 Simon says, 'Stand up and clap your hands once.'

9 Stamp your feet and wave your hand.

10 Simon says, 'Jump three times and say your name.'

11 Count to three.

12 Simon says, 'Touch your toes then stand up straight.'

13 Simon says, 'Hop three times then kneel on the floor.'

14 Stand up.

15 Simon says, 'Stand up and turn around.'

16 Simon says, 'Put your hands behind your back and close your eyes.'

17 Simon says, 'Open your eyes and sit on the floor.'

18 Put your hands in your lap.

19 Simon says, 'Put your hands on your head and stand up.'

20 Simon says, 'Put your hands by your side and face the window.'

It is round but you cannot eat it.	It can fly but it is not a bird.
It has four legs but it cannot walk.	It has a face and hands but cannot speak.
It cuts but it is not a knife.	It has a roof but it is not a house.
It has a trunk but it is not a tree.	You can sit on it but it is not a chair.

It flies but has no engine.

It lives in water but it is not a fish.

It has a handle but it is not a bag.

You can drive it but it is not a car.

You can read it but it is not a book.

You can dig with it but it is not a spade.

You can eat with it but it is not a knife.

It lives in a hole but it is not a rabbit.

It is round but you can't eat it	ball
It can fly but it is not a bird	plane, butterfly, bee, helicopter
It has four legs but it cannot walk	chair, table
It has a face and hands but cannot speak	clock
It cuts but it is not a knife	scissors
It has a roof but it is not a house	tent, caravan
It has a trunk but it is not a tree	elephant
You can sit on it but it is not a chair	bench, seat, sofa
It flies but has no engine	fly, bird, insect
It lives in water but it is not a fish	octopus, crab, frog
It has a handle but it is not a bag	cup, jug, brush
You can drive it but it is not a car	lorry, train, motorbike
You can read it but it is not a book	magazine, newpaper, letter
You can dig with it but it is not a spade	trowel
You can eat with it but it is not a knife	fork, spoon
It lives in a hole but it is not a rabbit	mouse, fox, mole, badger

b

s

ch

c

t

h

p

r

When can you play on the beach?	When do you have dinner?	When can you play in the paddling pool?	When can you see the moon?
When does the postman come?	When do you see stars in the sky?	When can you make a snowman?	When do you go to sleep?
When do the leaves fall off the trees?	When do you go in the playground?	When does Father Christmas come?	When can you see the sun?
When is the weather hot and sunny?	When do baby birds hatch?	When do you clean your teeth?	When do owls go hunting?
When does it sometimes snow?	When do you go to school?	When do you have breakfast?	When do you get up?

Special calendars give children a pictorial representation of days and weeks and the order in which events occur. They are most useful if they are tailor made for individual children and can be simplified, extended or adapted. They can be used:

- one day at a time

- to display two or three days

- for whole weeks or longer.

Basic features indicate morning and night and differentiate weekdays (school) from weekends (home).

You may want to add further permanent pictures of events which occur regularly. Otherwise you can build up a collection of stick-on pictures (using Velcro or Blu-tack) which can be added, moved or removed as necessary.

A sample of a weekday and a weekend day and some simple line drawings depicting typical school activities follows on the next two pages.

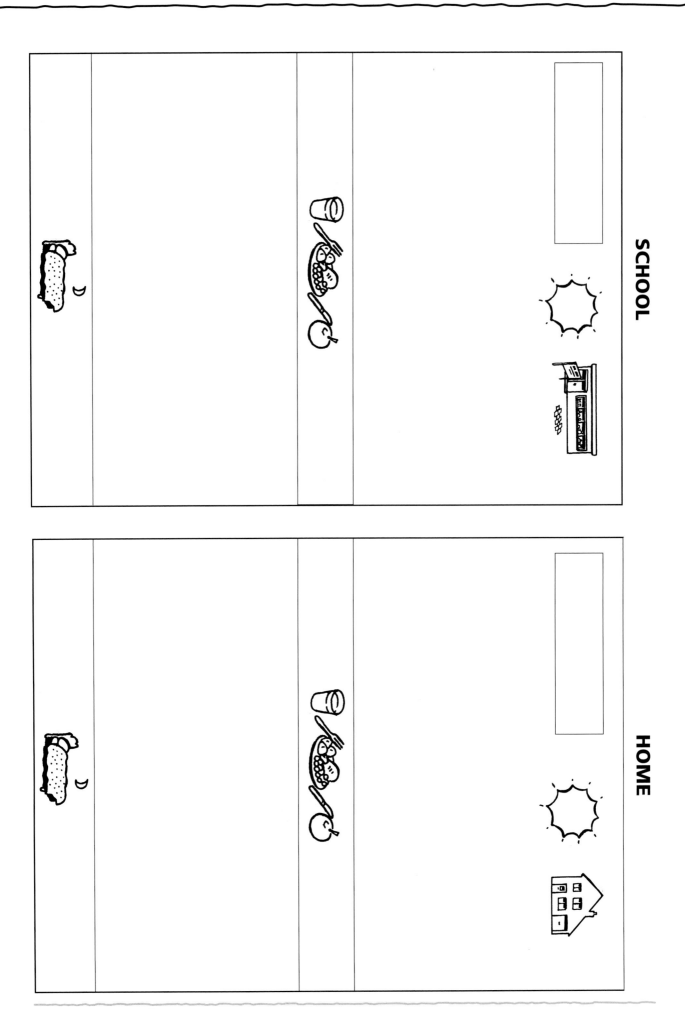

SCHOOL

HOME

Page 245

Show the child the sheet of pictures on the following page. Explain that these are pretend birthday presents. Say something about each of the pictures in turn and the child must guess which one it is.

1   This will be really useful in wet weather.

2   I can't wait to fly it on a windy day.

3   This has been on my reading list for ages.

4   It will need some batteries before it will work.

5   I shall get some brilliant pictures with this.

6   Oh good, my old ones have holes in the bottom.

7   Now I can text all my friends.

8   It will be just the thing for Auntie May's wedding.

9   Can we have a game after tea?

10   Please can you get me a jug to put them in?

Why do you wear a coat in the winter?

Why do you need to brush your teeth?

Why do birds have wings?

Why do people wear glasses?

Why are snakes dangerous?

Why do dogs bark?

Why do cars have wheels?

Why do we use an umbrella?

Why do we use a torch?

Why do we wear slippers?

Why do birds make a nest?

Why is one of the traffic lights red?

Why do we need a key?

Why do we put food in the oven?

Why do we need a fridge?

Why do we have a bath?

Why do we have brakes on a bike?

Why does Father Christmas carry a sack?

Why did Humpty Dumpty break into pieces?

Why do owls wake up at night?

Why did Cinderella have to go home from the ball?

Why did Red Riding Hood go to her granny's house?

Why did the wolf put granny's clothes on?

Why couldn't Cinderella go to the Ball?

Why did the Three Bears go for a walk?

Why did Goldilocks go upstairs?

Why was Jack's mother angry with him?

Why did Jack's mother throw the beans away?

Why did Goldilocks run home?

Why did Goldilocks leave daddy bear's porridge?

Why did the prince come to Cinderella's house?

Why did Little Red Riding Hood pick some flowers?

Why did the Three Little Pigs leave their mother's house?

Why did the first Little Pig ask the man for some straw?

Why did Jack cut down the beanstalk?

Why did Baby Bear cry?

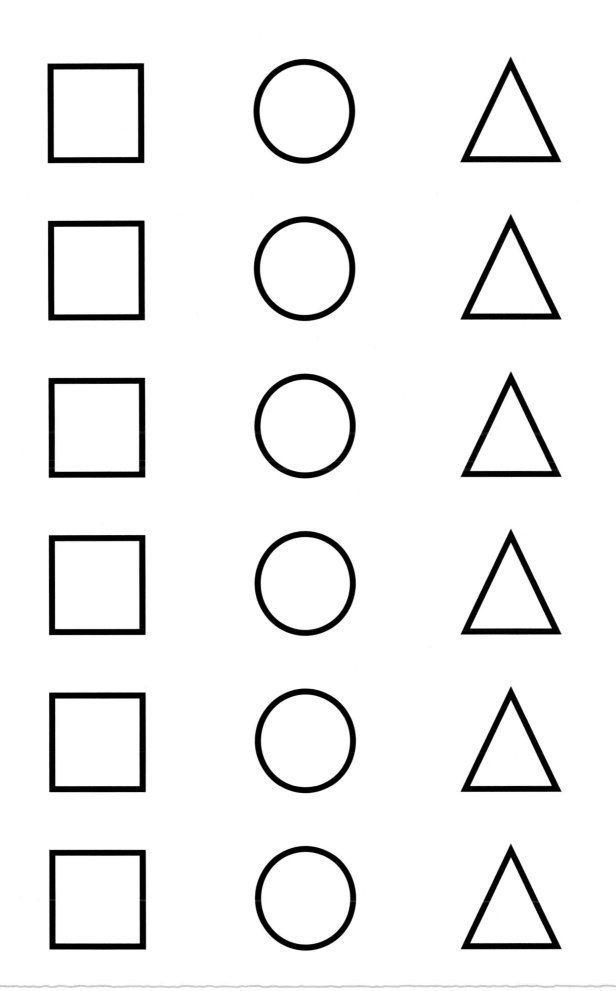

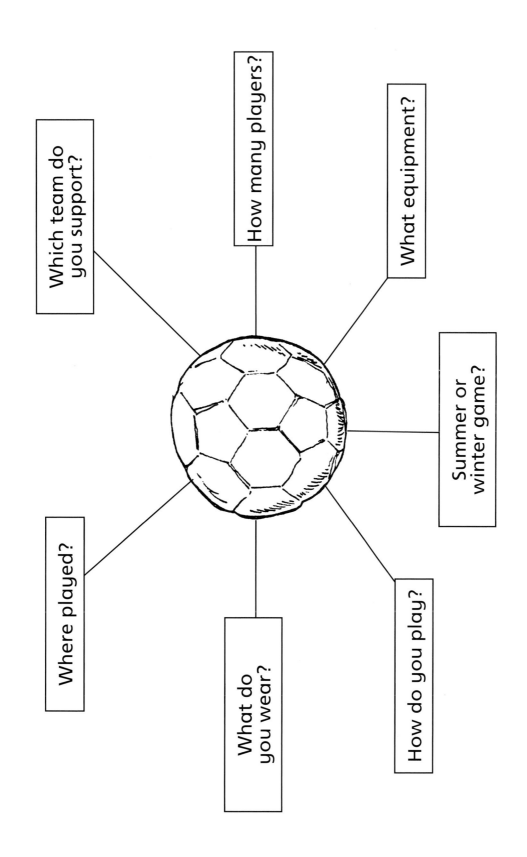

Which team do you support?

How many players?

What equipment?

Summer or winter game?

Where played?

What do you wear?

How do you play?

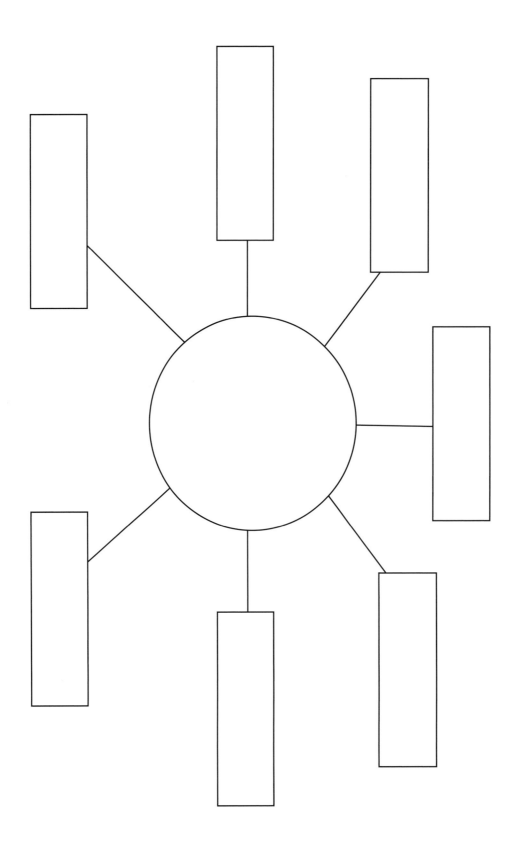

Someone who looks after your teeth	dentist
Someone who looks after sick people	doctor
Someone who builds houses	builder
Someone who teaches children	teacher
Someone who you pay in the supermarket	checkout staff
Someone who makes things with wood	carpenter
Someone who paints pictures	artist
Someone who acts in plays or on TV	actor
Someone who plays a musical instrument	musician
Someone who acts in films	film star
Someone who cuts people's hair	hairdresser
Someone who paints people's houses	painter
Someone who mends water pipes	plumber
Someone who keeps cows, pigs and sheep	farmer
Someone who looks after sick animals	vet
Someone who makes people laugh at the circus	clown
Someone who goes out in a boat to catch fish	fisherman
Someone who flies an aeroplane	pilot
Someone who is in the army	soldier
Someone who sails a ship	sailor
Someone who goes into space	astronaut
Someone who catches robbers	policeman
Someone who puts out fires	fire fighter
Someone who drives an ambulance	paramedic

USEFUL BOOKS

Books are most useful as language teaching tools if they have beautiful or funny pictures, or if they are interesting stories. Other useful features are the inclusion of repetition and rhyme. We have listed just a very few of the books which we have found popular and motivating, and which can be used for a variety of different purposes. Examples would be *Where's Spot?* for question words, the *Mr Men* books for descriptive words, *Look Behind You!* for place words. You need to refer to your teaching target and choose your book accordingly. Many of the books listed will be in Reception and Year 1 libraries.

GENERAL VOCABULARY

Usborne Look and Say books

My Very First Books, Eric Carle, Penguin Books

Dorling Kindersley Big Books

Ladybird Talkabout Books

Richard Scarry books, Harper Collins Children's Books

Dr Seuss Beginner Books

The Mr Men series, Roger Hargreaves, Egmont Books

Charlie and Lola's Opposites, Lauren Child, Orchard Books

Maisy's Amazing Big Book of Words, Lucy Cousins, Walker Books

100 Best Loved Nursery Rhymes, Belinda Gallagher, Miles Kelly Publishing

EARLIEST 'STARTER' STORIES

Maisy Books, Lucy Cousins, Walker Books

Spot Books, Eric Hill, Puffin Books

The Very Hungry Caterpillar, Eric Carle, Penguin Books

Dear Zoo, Rod Campbell, Campbell Books

Oh Dear! Rod Campbell, Campbell Books

The Blue Balloon, Mick Inkpen, Hodder Children's Books

Miffy Books, Dick Bruna, Egmont Books

Angry Ladybird, Eric Carle, Puffin Books

It's Mine, Rod Campbell, Campbell Books

Fat, Thin and Other Opposites, Ingrid Gordon, Barron Educational Series

POPULAR STORIES

Ladybird Favourite Tales (includes all the old favourites such as *The Gingerbread Man, The Enormous Turnip, Goldilocks and the Three Bears*)

Shhh! Sally Grindley and Peter Utton, Hodder Children's Books

The Tiger who Came to Tea, Judith Kerr, Harper Collins Children's Books

The Gruffalo, Julia Donaldson and Axel Scheffler, Macmillan Children's Books

The Smartest Giant in Town, Julia Donaldson and Axel Scheffler, Macmillan Children's Books

We're Going on a Bear Hunt, Michael Rosen and Helen Oxenbury, Walker Books

The Runaway Train, Benedict Blathwayt, Red Fox Books

The Little Blue Car, Gwen Grant, Orchard Books

Snake Supper, Alan Durant and Ant Parker, Collins Picture Lions

Peace at Last, Jill Murphy, Walker Books

Dinosaur Roar, P and H Stickland, Ragged Bears Books

Look Behind You! Tony Maddox, Orchard Books

Wibbly Pig books, Mick Inkpen, Hodder Children's Books

Where the Wild Things Are, Maurice Sendak, Red Fox Books

Kipper books, Mick Inkpen, Hodder Children's Books

Mog books, Judith Kerr, Harper Collins Children's Books

Percy the Parkkeeper books, Nick Butterworth, Harper Collins Children's Books

Six Dinner Sid, Inga Moore, Hodder Children's Books

Elmer books, David McKee, Andersen Press

The Snail and the Whale, Julia Donaldson, Macmillan Children's Books

The Little Boat, Kathy Henderson and Patrick Benson, Walker Books

Little Bear, Martin Waddell, Walker Books

SUPPLIERS OF GAMES

Match a Balloon　　　Ravensburger Games
　　　　　　　　　　　www.ravensburger.com

Mousie Mousie　　　　Rocket Toys and Games
　　　　　　　　　　　PO Box 37 Tadcaster LS24 9XD, UK
　　　　　　　　　　　Tel: +44 (0)870 012 9090

ColorCards® series　　Speechmark Publishing Ltd
Early Actions　　　　　70 Alston Drive, Bradwell Abbey, Milton Keynes MK13 9HG, UK
Early Opposites　　　　Tel: +44 (0)1908 326 944
Occupations　　　　　www.speechmark.net
What's Different?
What's Wrong?
　(revised edition 2007)

Jolly Phonics　　　　Jolly Learning Ltd
　　　　　　　　　　　Tailours House, High Road, Chigwell, Essex IG7 6DL,UK
　　　　　　　　　　　Tel: + 44 (0)20 8501 0405
　　　　　　　　　　　www.jollylearning.co.uk

Why Because　　　　Black Sheep Press
　　　　　　　　　　　67 Middleton, Cowling, Keighley BD22 0DQ, UK
　　　　　　　　　　　Tel: +44 (0)1535 631346
　　　　　　　　　　　www.blacksheep-epress.com

Pairs　　　　　　　LDA
Things That Go Together　Abbeygate House, East Road, Cambridge CB1 1DB, UK
　　　　　　　　　　　Tel: +44 (0)845 120 4776
　　　　　　　　　　　www.LDAlearning.com

DICTIONARY OF TERMS

adjective   A word that describes a noun (eg *pink* dress, *pretty* girl, *big* dog).

adverb   A word that describes a verb (eg walk *slowly*, stroking *gently*).

article   A word used with a noun to clarify what it refers to (eg *a*, *the*, *those*).

articulation   The movements of the speech organs (eg lips, tongue, soft palate) to make sounds.

attainment   Level of skill acquired in such things as reading, writing, numeracy.

auditory discrimination   The ability to distinguish between similar sounds or words.

auditory memory   The immediate recall of heard information.

auxiliary verb   A word linked to the main verb to indicate tense (eg *is* jumping, *has* eaten, *will* go).

blending   Combining sounds to make words (eg c-a-t, sh-o-p).

centiles   A way of comparing test scores against an average group of 100 people of the same age. Fifth centile means only 5 per cent of children would score at or below this level. Ninetieth centile means 90 per cent of children would score at or below this level; therefore the child is in the top 10 per cent of his age group.

clause   A secondary part of a sentence which contains a verb (eg Fetch the book *your mum sent in with you*).

cloze procedure   Leaving gaps in a sentence, to be filled in.

cluster   A group of consonants (eg str, thr, pl, sw).

cognitive abilities   Thinking, reasoning, problem-solving skills (intellectual functioning).

communication   The exchange of facts, ideas and feelings between people, by any system.

comprehension   Understanding, specifically of language.

conceptual ability   Ability to understand and make sense of the world as a result of understanding of concepts.

consolidation   Going over work again to make sure the child really knows it.

consonants   Letters of the alphabet other than vowels, ie not a, e, i, o, u. y is classed as a consonant when it begins a word (eg *y*ellow), but as a semi-vowel when it comes at the end (eg funn*y*).

context   Words that come before and/or after a particular word that help to indicate its meaning, or the circumstance in which an event occurs.

differentiation   Work being matched to the child's ability. Enabling the child to demonstrate knowledge using alternative means (eg the computer).

discourse   A continuous episode of language (especially spoken) involving several sentences.

discrepancy   The difference between a child's general ability and his level of attainment in reading, writing or numeracy.

dysfluency See *stammering*.

dyslexia Specific difficulty in learning to read, not due to general learning difficulties.

echolalia Copying words and phrases without understanding them.

ellipsis A concise, sometimes incomplete, utterance which can be understood because the listener knows the context (eg 'Most mornings' in reply to the question 'Do you ever go swimming?'). The non-elliptical answer would be 'Yes, I go swimming most mornings.'

expressive language Spoken language.

figurative language See *idiom* and *metaphor*.

fine motor skills Skills involving finger and hand control (eg pencil control, grasping, gripping).

fluency The smooth joining of sounds, syllables, words and phrases during spoken language.

fricative A speech sound in which there is no complete stoppage of air (eg the tongue approaches the hard palate but does not touch it, so that the air 'slides' out as in 'sss'). Other fricatives are f, v, sh, z, zh (the sound in measure).

fronting Making speech sounds further forward in the mouth than they should be (eg 't' for 'c' and so 'tar' for car, and 'd' for 'g' and so 'dame' for game). Typical of immature speech.

functional language The way language is used practically and effectively in everyday situations.

generalisation Learning to apply newly learnt skills to different tasks, situations or contexts.

global/general learning difficulties Overall difficulty in learning.

grammar Rules of language structure.

gross motor skills Running, climbing, balancing, walking, catching, throwing, etc.

hearing Detection of sound via the ears.

homonyms Words which sound the same but have different meanings (eg *bare/bear*). May also be spelt the same (eg *bear* the pain, grizzly *bear*).

idiom An expression that has become accepted as having a certain meaning, although this may not be evident from the actual words (eg 'She has green fingers').

inference Understanding of things implied but not spelt out such as 'Rover barked and wagged his tail.' The listener infers that Rover is a dog.

intonation The rising and falling of pitch or melody in speech.

jargon Meaningless strings of words, nonsense words.

language An organised set of spoken or written words, signs, pictures or symbols used to communicate.

language delay Language development that is following a normal pattern but at a slower rate than the average.

language disorder Language that is developing abnormally.

lexicon Word store. See also *vocabulary*.

listening   Attending to sounds or speech.

literal interpretation   Taking humorous, sarcastic or figurative language at its face value (eg expecting animals to descend from the sky if someone says 'It's raining cats and dogs').

metalinguistics   Thinking about how words and language behave.

metaphor   An imaginative way of describing something by calling it something else (eg 'His fingers were blocks of ice').

morpheme   The smallest distinctive unit of grammar (eg a plural *s*, a tense marker *ed*).

morphology   The way words are changed to alter meaning by the addition of morphemes, (eg car/cars, jump/jumped).

non-verbal performance (non-verbal skills)   Measure of child's ability to think and reason when tasks are presented visually, not through language, and need practical problem-solving skills (eg jigsaws).

non-verbal reasoning   Practical problem-solving skills (eg self-monitoring, learning from mistakes, and forming hypotheses).

normative assessment   Assessment allowing the child's score to be compared with the scores of children of the same age, indicating whether his score is above or below average.

noun   A naming word such as a person (*Jo*), a place (*Rome*) or an object (*table*).

onset   The sound corresponding to the initial consonants in syllables (eg *s*-ing, *str*-ing, *m*-other).

oral-motor skills   The ability to carry out purposeful movements of tongue, lips and muscles of the mouth.

phoneme   A speech sound (eg the sound of *m*, *sh*, *oo*).

phonetics   The system of symbols used by speech & language therapists, among others, to transcribe speech patterns.

phonics   Linking sounds to letters.

phonology   The way in which sounds are organised in speech and language.

phonological awareness   The recognition of sounds, sound systems and sound patterns in words, and the ability to manipulate and remember them. Includes awareness of syllable structure and rhyme.

phonological disorder   Difficulty in recognising sounds and sound sequences, resulting in wrong use of sounds in speech and often difficulty in reading and spelling.

phrase   A few words together which have meaning, but do not contain a verb (eg 'the house on the hill', 'the brown dog').

pictogram   A written symbol used to convey a meaning.

plosive   A speech sound in which there is a brief complete stoppage of the air flow through the speech organs (eg *p*, *b*, *t*, *d*, *k*, *g*).

pragmatics   The social, interactive and empathetic aspects of communication, including non-verbal skills (eg gesture, facial expression).

preposition   A word used with a noun or pronoun to indicate place (*at* home), position (*in* the car), time (*on* Sunday), or means (*by* train).

pronoun   A word used instead of a noun (eg *I*, *me*, *her*, *his*, *it*).

prosody   The rhythm and tune of speech, including intonation, pitch, speed, stress and loudness.

receptive language   See *comprehension*.

rhyme   When the rimes of words sound the same (eg l-*ine*/m-*ine*, pl-*ate*/w-*ait*, c-*alf*/l-*augh*).

rhythm   The pattern produced by stressing words and syllables in sentences (eg 'The *dan*cing *bear* went *up* the *stair*').

rime   The sound corresponding to the remaining letters in a syllable after the onset (eg sh-*op*, cr-*owd*).

segmenting   Separating individual sounds or syllables in words (eg c-r-o-p, um-bre-lla).

self-esteem   A measure of the difference between how a person wants to be and how they see themselves. If the gap between these is large, the person has low self-esteem.

semantics   The meaning conveyed by words and sentences.

sentence   A set of words complete in itself, containing a verb (eg 'The boy rode his bike').

sequencing   Arranging words, pictures or other things in correct or logical order.

short-term auditory memory   See *auditory memory*.

sight vocabulary   The understanding of written words by their general appearance rather than by awareness of their phonic components.

simile   Description of something by comparing it with something else (eg as brave as *a lion*).

sound system   The way a person organises and uses speech sounds when talking.

spatial   In language, indicates that a word has to do with position rather than time (eg 'Find the *first* picture in the line' as opposed to 'Get your books out *first*').

specific learning difficulties   Specific difficulties in reading, writing, spelling or numeracy. The difficulties are not typical of the child's general level of performance.

speech   The spoken medium for transmitting language.

stammering   Difficulty in producing fluent speech. May involve repetition of sounds, syllables or phrases, and/or total blocks when no sound can be produced for a brief time.

standard score   A test score compared to those achieved by a reference group of children of the same age, indicating whether the child's score is above or below average.

stopping   Making a short sound (plosive) instead of a gliding sound (fricative), (eg *p* instead of *f* ['pish' for fish] or *t* for *s* ['tock' for sock]).

stuttering   American term for stammering.

syllables   The beats in words (eg um-bre-lla).

synonyms   Words with the same meaning (eg high, lofty, tall).

syntax   The rules governing the way in which words are put together in sentences.

temporal   In language, indicates that a word has to do with time rather than space (eg 'Do your writing *first*' rather than 'Put your coat on the *first* peg').

tense   The form of a verb indicating past, present, future, conditional (eg I ran/was running/ am running/run/will run/would run).

unintelligible   Speech largely or wholly impossible to understand.

utterance   A word or sequence of words spoken in a specific context.

verb   An action (doing) word (eg run, jump, read).

verbal comprehension   See *comprehension*.

verbal reasoning   Using language to solve problems.

verbal understanding   See *comprehension*.

vocabulary   The collection of words an individual understands and may (or may not) be able to use.

vowels   Letters of the alphabet other than consonants, ie a, e, i, o, u. y is classed as a semi-vowel when it occurs at the end of words.

word finding   The ability to find the word you want from your word-store (lexicon).

word finding difficulty   Particular difficulty in retrieving even familiar words from your lexicon.

word level   The number of key words you must understand to interpret a sentence accurately (eg *fetch* the *red book* from the *big cupboard*).

Complementary titles from Speechmark ...

Developing Baseline Communication Skills

Catherine Delamain & Jill Spring

Developing Baseline Communication Skills is a timely practical resource designed to fit closely with the baseline assessments now being introduced into schools. It contains a programme of games and activities aimed at fostering personal and social development, and promoting language and early literacy skills. This resource seeks to address some of these problems and offers games and activities suitable for four- to five-year-olds in nursery education, playgroups, reception classes and those attending speech and language therapy clinics. There are two hundred games and activities, graded into levels of difficulty for whole classes or smaller groups.

Speaking, Listening & Understanding: Games for Young Children

Catherine Delamain & Jill Spring

Written by two experienced speech & language therapists, who have worked extensively alongside mainstream teachers, this book provides activities that are both teacher and child friendly. It contains a collection of graded games and activities designed to foster the speaking, listening and understanding skills of children aged from 5 to 7. The activities are divided into two main areas: **Understanding Spoken Language**: Following Instructions; Getting the Main Idea; Thinking Skills; Developing Vocabulary; Understanding Inference; and **Using Spoken Language**: Narrating; Describing; Explaining; Predicting; Playing with Words.

School Start: Programmes for Language & Sound Awareness

Catherine de la Bedoyere & Catharine Lowry

School Start is an early intervention programme to enhance children's language and sound awareness skills during reception year in mainstream primary schools. Designed to be carried out by teaching assistants, under the guidance of the school's inclusion coordinator and in close collaboration with class teachers, parents and speech & language therapists, each programme consists of 30 weekly group activities split into six-week blocks. Each block has clearly written objectives that are linked to the National Curriculum Foundation Stage.

Speechmark

Complementary titles from Speechmark ...

Riddles, Rhyme & Alliteration: Listening Exercises Based on Phonics

Jane Turner

Riddles, Rhyme and Alliteration is a practical resource that encourages children to concentrate, listen to and discriminate between different speech sounds. Written for teachers of children aged 5–7 years, it can also be used with older children who have listening and auditory discrimination difficulties, poor listening skills, and mild to moderate hearing loss or 'glue ear'. Each section is based on a particular phoneme and contains a wide variety of exercises and games as well as a puzzle worksheet that allows the child to work independently.

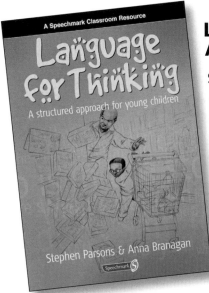

Language for Thinking: A Structured Approach for Young Children

Stephen Parsons & Anna Branagan

This photocopiable resource provides a clear structure to assist teachers, SENCOs, learning support assistants and speech & language therapists in developing children's language from the concrete to the abstract. It is based on fifty picture and verbal scenarios that can be used flexibly with a wide range of ages and abilities. It is quick, practical and easy to use in the classroom and can be used with individual children, in small groups or can form the basis of a literacy lesson or speech & language therapy session.

Developing Language Concepts: Programmes for School-Aged Children

Bridget Burrows

This book is a valuable resource for all speech & language therapists, teachers and support assistants working with children in schools and community clinics. It provides practical, step-by-step photocopiable programmes to help with specific language concepts, such as amount, colour, size, time and shape. The programmes are intended for speech & language therapists to copy and send to the school where staff can deliver the programmes, although they can be used by the therapist themselves. The exercises can be personalised for each child and are graded so that the therapist can select and copy the sheets relevant to the child's needs. Each programme introduces the concept, teaches it and then checks to see if the child understands it.